THE RISE OF URBAN AMERICA

ADVISORY EDITOR
Richard C. Wade

PROFESSOR OF AMERICAN HISTORY
UNIVERSITY OF CHICAGO

SATELLITE CITIES

A STUDY OF INDUSTRIAL SUBURBS

Graham Romeyn Taylor

ARNO PRESS
&
The New York Times

NEW YORK · 1970

Reprint Edition 1970 by Arno Press Inc.

Reprinted from a copy in The Newark Public Library

LC# 70-112576
ISBN 0-405-02478-9

THE RISE OF URBAN AMERICA
ISBN for complete set 0-405-02430-4

Manufactured in the United States of America

SATELLITE CITIES

173A

NATIONAL MUNICIPAL LEAGUE SERIES

SATELLITE CITIES

A STUDY OF INDUSTRIAL SUBURBS

BY

GRAHAM ROMEYN TAYLOR

ILLUSTRATED

NEW YORK AND LONDON
D. APPLETON AND COMPANY
1915

TO MY FATHER

GRAHAM TAYLOR

FOREWORD

Congestion, with all that it means in choked streets, dark work rooms and high taxes, has been forcing factories to our city limits and beyond. To direct attention to this process and particularly to its civic consequences is the purpose of this book. It endeavors to set forth the opportunity in these outskirts for applying the technique which is being developed and the idealism which is finding expression in the new science of town planning. For while industrial managers have shown extraordinary foresight, skill and ingenuity in the arrangement of their plants in the outlying areas, no such expert planning has gone into the accompanying community development.

These pages are not an attempt to solve the resulting complex problems. They are an effort to set forth definite facts from typical communities where these problems and the general situation which embodies them are seen in bold outline. The writer went about his investigation with no preconceived opinions or theories to substantiate, but with human values first in his mind and the common welfare uppermost in his purpose. Criticism of civic shortcomings on the part of the industrial control and public authorities is made not so much to place responsibility as to point the way toward constructive progress. The main thing to be

desired is the coöperation of public officials, working
people, industrial leaders and enlightened citizens to
secure better living and truer democracy.

Most of the material in this volume appeared first
as a series of articles in *The Survey*. To its editor,
Paul U. Kellogg, whose coöperation during the collection and arrangement of the data and whose editorial help were of the utmost value, the author acknowledges his great debt. Miss Jane Addams'
courtesy in permitting the use of a paper she originally
read before the Chicago Woman's Club and the
Twentieth Century Club of Boston is especially appreciated. For suggestions in manuscript revision
the author is grateful to Francis Hackett, formerly
literary editor of the Chicago *Evening Post* and now
on the staff of *The New Republic*. To those who
contributed to the symposium in the appendix, and to
those who helped in the field work, the revision of
chapters, and the preparation of maps, diagrams and
illustrations, the author also extends his thanks.

More deeply than he can well express, he feels
what he owes to years of companionship with his
father, whose work at Chicago Commons and out-
reaching influence in civic and industrial relations
have unfailingly emphasized the human point of view.
This companionship, this work and influence, have constantly strengthened a faith in that democracy which
is essential if citizen and worker are to gain all that
should come through the community's guidance of its
own growth.

INTRODUCTION

Several years ago Graham Romeyn Taylor, then, as now, one of the editorial staff of *The Survey,* visited the various communities which had grown up in the vicinity of the larger cities of the country. He saw the several situations with the eyes of a trained observer of civic affairs, and possessing a strong reportorial instinct, he proceeded to tell what he saw to the readers of *The Survey.* He was not content, however, merely to tell what he saw. He was keen to find out what it all meant, and start his readers thinking about the conditions. This he proceeded to do under the happily chosen title " Satellite Cities."

It seemed to the Editor of the National Municipal League Series that these illuminating papers should have a more permanent form. And so it was proposed that they be gathered and rounded out into a volume and made available to students of urban problems and of industry. This task Mr. Taylor has performed with skill and effectiveness, and has brought home the lessons of experience to those dealing with the involved questions of manufacture, land, labor and population.

These " made-to-order " cities—for " satellite cities " are really made to order, not thrown off the parent body at a given moment—not only have problems of their own, and serious ones, but they have lessons for the city planner and the student of the larger municipal problems. We can see in the experience of these cities how carefully made plans work out in practice. Here we study in detail the results of policies which have been urged for the larger centers. For, as Mr. Taylor points out, they have " come to share in the common lot."

Mr. Taylor's volume, which is the first in this series to be illustrated, will form an admirable complement to John Nolen's volume, " City Planning," which is now in press. It might be given the sub-title of " Applied City Planning," for the developments which are described are just that.

The discussion of an " Employer's Utopia " leads to the inclusion of a parenthetical chapter by Jane Addams, an analysis of the results of the late George M. Pullman's effort to care in a fatherly way for the great army of employees necessary to build his cars. Miss Addams and Mr. Taylor both face the problem involved in the attempt to impose good government, which is the idea of so many, but which so far has not worked out in our American communities. These may not be wholly democratic; but they are democratic in their tendencies, and to an increasing degree they are preferring democracy to efficiency, although striving for both.

CLINTON ROGERS WOODRUFF.

August, 1915.

SUMMARY

CHAPTER I

THE OUTER RINGS OF INDUSTRY

City planning as process — Industry seeks the city's edge — Pullman and other pioneers — Made-to-order towns incidents in a vast movement — Its meaning in workers' lives — Ingenuity and foresight in factory arrangement, not applied to town planning — Land values and home ownership — Transportation and community life — Irregular work serious in a one industry town — Attempt to take workers away from centers of labor " trouble "— Company control and local politics — Industrial exodus and civic opportunity.

CHAPTER II

REDISCOVERING AN EMPLOYER'S UTOPIA

Pullman and its meaning — The " model " town in the eighties — Paternalism broken up by annexation to Chicago, the strike of 1894 and court decision against company holding of real state — Change from company to public control — Housing — Population and racial shift — Steel cars bring new processes — Work and wages — Civic conditions — Adjacent " Bumtown "— Old and new in recreation, schools and health — Pullman's place in Chicago's plan — How the people felt toward the company — Civic independence and ward politics — Chicago's first socialist alderman — Genius of great men and faith in democracy.

CHAPTER III

A MODERN LEAR. *A Parenthetical Chapter by Jane Addams*

The industrial tragedy at Pullman — Its lesson for to-day — King Lear and a captain of industry — Ingratitude in chil-

dren and employees — The benevolent autocrat — Good deeds
in place of human relationship— The sheltered daughter finds
a larger life — Pullman employees emerge in the labor movement — Individual virtues and social ethics — The self-
righteous philanthropist in a changing age — Brotherhood of
the workers must also recognize the employer —"The consent
of men " in industrial relations and social progress.

CHAPTER IV

INDUSTRY'S ESCAPE FROM CONGESTION

Trend of factories to the outskirts more important than spectacular company towns — Workers left behind at Cincinnati
— Commuting from city tenements to suburban plants —
No loss of workers though hours and wages unchanged —
A well-planned " factory colony "— No planning for people
— Land cheap for plants but high for homes — Making room
for wage-earners in a residential suburb — The Schmidlapp
housing experiment — Coöperative housekeeping — Where
" bright lights " are not shining, neighborhood recreation must
be planned — Public spirit and the suburb — The challenge of
the " factory colony " to the scheming of community life.

CHAPTER V

ECONOMIC GAIN AND CIVIC ISOLATION

An " east side " in the west — St. Louis and her Illinois
satellites — Usual economic advantages — The " arbitrary " on coal — Civic barriers in a great river and a state
line — Creating a town and its land values — Meager recreation but short hours of work — Three eight-hour shifts instead of two of twelve hours in steel plants — The companies
save money — What leisure means to men — Trade unions —
A socialist mayor — Frank differences but no bitterness —
Greater isolation for foreigners —" Hungary Hollow "—Bulgarians and Macedonians — Their neglected conditions —
The need for civic unity in a metropolitan industrial district.

CHAPTER VI

A CITY BY DECREE

Creating a city by fiat — Gary's sand dunes and destiny —
The chosen spot of a master industry — Bending nature to

the needs of steel — Twenty square miles of elbow-room —
Scientific plant arrangement and civic rule-o'-thumb — The
works gate as a town focus — A gridiron street scheme —
Kidnapping towns — Strategy for industrial stress — Industry holds the lake front against the people's use — Fundamental utilities — Company houses — Cement construction —
" Hunkyville "— Inadequate housing for immigrants — The
framework ready for life.

CHAPTER VII

THE EMERGENCE OF DEMOCRACY

The human side of the steel city — Wholesale provision for
community life — The town's life seeks its own expression —
Frontier conditions and pioneer spirit— Gary's people — Immigrants and real-estate exploitation — High rents for shacks
— Needed housing regulation — Living costs — Eighteen
times as much for police as for health — Saloons — Labor
organization — The town denies a trolley franchise to steel
men — Turbulent politics and civic independence Schools
and a man — The community's big achievement — Schools
rival steel in making Gary famous — Growth of community
coöperation — Tonnage methods of industry inadequate for
life.

CHAPTER VIII

TOWN BUILDING BY PRIVATE ENTERPRISE

The key city of the " new South " Three types of industrial
satellites — A down-at-the-heel cotton mill village — A dreary
steel town of the eighties — A " model town " through a real-
estate company — Fairfield's modern plan — Applying invention to streets and houses — Civic center and community institutions — A zoning scheme — Large lots and attractive
bungalows — Putting thought into back yards — Neighborhood coöperation — Influence of an example — Where the
town falls short — No houses for low-paid labor — Real-estate speculation at the workers' expense — But plants escape
taxes by jogs in a boundary — Trolley franchise granted in
perpetuity before the town was born — Contrasts with the
English Birmingham — The need for civic statesmanship.

CHAPTER IX

COMMUNITY PLANNING

The speed of industry's outward thrust — A vast unnoticed movement — Exploring the city's outer rings — Common welfare at stake — Left to industrial captains or real-estate speculation — Problems which challenge community foresight and intelligence — Applying constructive genius to outlying areas — The English garden suburbs — Scheming living and livelihood — The co-partnership tenants' principle — Land values for the community — Tenants' advantages — Better than individual home ownership — Success of the co-partnership tenants' associations — Adaptability to America — England's town planning act — Legislation for suburban development — Public guidance for city growth — Democracy's doorway from politics into industry and everyday life.

APPENDIX

SATELLITE CITIES FROM VARIOUS VIEWPOINTS

" The Human Emphasis " by Charles Mulford Robinson — " The Way Out " by George B. Ford —" Co-partnership Housing " by Henry Vivian — " Factors in Plant Efficiency " by Irving T. Bush —" Planning for Metropolitan Needs " by Andrew Wright Crawford —" Factory and Home " by John Nolen —" The Employers' Part " by Flavel Shurtleff —" From the Housing Point of View " by John Ihlder.

CONTENTS

LIST OF ILLUSTRATIONS

SATELLITE CITIES

AT THE CITY'S RIM

PLACE YOUR HAND OVER THE TOP HALF OF THE PIC-
TURE. YOU SEE THE CORN STUBBLE AND STRAGGLING
ORCHARD OF AN OLD PRAIRIE FARM. PLACE YOUR HAND
OVER THE LOWER HALF AND THERE STAND THE TANKS,
FACTORY BUILDINGS AND STACKS OF A HUGE INDUSTRIAL
PLANT. THESE ARE NOT TWO PICTURES BUT ONE, THE
TRANSFORMATION WHICH IS GOING ON AS INDUSTRY IS
MOVING OUT TO THE OPEN. THIS BOOK DEALS WITH HU-
MAN BEINGS SWEPT OUT BY THE PROCESS.

CHAPTER I

THE OUTER RINGS OF INDUSTRY

" BACK to the land " has come to mean more than the migration of a few tenement dwellers to farms. The big opportunity for the escape from crowded cities is through the wholesale removal of the work which city people do. Huge industrial plants are uprooting themselves bodily from the cities. With households, small stores, saloons, lodges, churches, schools clinging to them like living tendrils, they set themselves down ten miles away in the open.

While we spend years of effort in reconstructing our civic centers, only to have our schemes stalled by costly obstructions of brick and mortar and suspended by condemnation proceedings, city extension as a process is going on every week and every month on the edges of our cities.

Towns made to order entirely, or with some little village as a core, snatch bundles of papers from the morning trains, smudge new postmarks over sheet after sheet of red postage stamps, edge their way into the telephone toll books and the freight tariffs, scrawl their names on the tags of new-coming immigrants at

Ellis Island and become part and parcel of up-and-doing municipal America before most of their slower going sister cities have even heard of their existence.

From the middle of Philadelphia, several departments of the Baldwin Locomotive Works have been shunted out into a small suburb. Flint, Michigan, two hours from Detroit, has been seized as the place for huge automobile factories. While the population was trebling in the first three years, several hundred operatives had to be housed in tents throughout one summer. A big corn-products plant moved from the middle of Chicago to the near-by prairies and a " glucose city," Argo, started up. It occupies part of a tract of ten square miles, which one promoting company is developing as an " industrial district " and into which Chicago has already emptied more than two dozen establishments. Just outside Cincinnati a residential suburb, Norwood, is now the home of a score of manufacturing concerns. Impelled partly by the arbitrary tolls charged on coal carried across the Mississippi River, industrial plants have moved over the bridges from St. Louis and founded a group of new towns in Illinois. The Standard Oil Company, a few years ago, poured out $3,500,000 on the bank of the Missouri a few miles from Kansas City, and the town of Sugar Creek sprang up. Yonkers long since lost its staid old character in a smother of hat and carpet factories. The metropolitan manufacturing district stretches out in belts and flanges from New York into

FROM CITY CENTER TO SUBURB
Old and New Plants, Corn Products Refining Company, Chicago.
3

Long Island, Staten Island and New Jersey, while eastern Massachusetts is a mosaic of mill towns. In some sections of the South scarcely a city of any size lacks one or more satellites thrumming with spindle and shuttle.

Gary, with its population nearing 50,000, where in 1906 there were only rolling sand dunes covered with scrub oak, is thus seen to be but the largest and most spectacular example of the far-reaching industrial exodus. Far-reaching and fast-moving, for Gary had scarcely attained four-year-old dignity when work started on a still newer member of the United States Steel Corporation's brood of steel towns — Fairfield, first known as Corey, on the edge of Birmingham, Alabama. On the heels of Fairfield came the news that more millions and another plant would found another steel town near Duluth.

This industrial exodus from city center to suburb was first seen conspicuously in the establishment of Pullman and Homestead in the early eighties. These two places were by no means the only forerunners. South Omaha, for example, in 1883, sprang up around the stockyards at a railway junction so rapidly as to win the name " Magic City." These exceptional towns, suddenly created at the dictate of pioneer master minds of the new industrialism, thrilled the popular imagination.

But they were freshets where the present movement has taken on the proportions of a big sweeping current. It is spreading through suburban areas as well as creating made-to-order towns. The Census Bureau has gathered data from thirteen "industrial districts," each of which covers a large city and its vicinity.

Number of workers increased:

In large cities 40.8 per cent.

In surrounding zones 97.7 per cent.

TEN YEARS' GROWTH OF SUBURBAN INDUSTRY

For twelve of them the statistics are available for the years 1899, 1904 and 1909. From 1899 to 1904 the number of persons employed in industries in the surrounding zones increased 32.8 per cent., while within the limits of the central cities there was only 14.9 per cent. increase. From 1904 to 1909 the increase in the surrounding zones was 48.8 per cent., and within the cities 22.5 per cent. But taking the figures for the whole decade, the increase in the surrounding zones was 97.7 per cent., and in the cities but 40.8 per cent.

Many reasons are readily apparent for the location of these new industrial communities. The impulse toward cheap land, low taxes and elbow-room throws them out from the large centers of population. These are the centrifugal forces. The centripetal forces are equally powerful and bind them as satellites beyond the outer rings of the mother city. Even the towns which, like Gary, have attained a considerable measure of self-sufficiency and lie perhaps across state boundaries are bound by strong economic ties. Through switch-yards and belt-lines, practically all the railroad facilities developed during years of growth, which are at the disposal of a downtown establishment, are at the service of the industry in the suburb. It means much to be within easy reach of at least one large market for finished product. Proximity to a big labor market is a more important factor.

The purpose of these pages, however, is not primarily to discuss the economic causes which lead to the sudden investment of large sums of capital in establishing suburban plants. It is rather to explore a little way into what the movement means for the great numbers of work-people who are caught up and swept out with it. How do these new work places pan out as communities of people living together — families, neighbors, citizens?

The census bulletin referred to sums up the industrial exodus in numbers of manufacturing establishments, in value of products, etc. From the standpoint of the common welfare, it should be reckoned also in terms of citizenship and human values. What of health and housing? Of leisure and income to make it count? Of playgrounds and schools? Of living costs? Of city government, politics and civic spirit?

There is a public challenge in the very fact that in these localities civic and industrial conditions are being created brand-new, on a wholesale scale, without the handicaps and restrictions which high land values and prior improvements impose on every effort to reconstruct the congested centers. Are we turning these advantages to account? In our general municipal development we pay more and more heed to the counsel of city planner, housing expert and sanitarian. We struggle to reshape our rigid, old-established conditions to fit newer and more workable molds, just as the manufacturer has to tear out, rebuild and build higher if he stays in the midst of congestion while his business expands.

But have we set ourselves to inquire whether these made-to-order industrial cities, involving living conditions for thousands of people, are so shaped at the outset? In the planning of the great suburban industrial plant, marvelous skill and foresight are shown in adapting buildings and machinery to the processes through which stuff becomes finished product. Is a similar skill and foresight applied to the development of the things through which houses may become homes, a construction camp a community, and livelihood life? Apparently the answer is often in the negative.

Whereas in the Gary plant, for example, the utmost ingenuity was shown in scheming out shortcuts, the street planning of the town was on the old checker-board system. The placing of the blast furnaces was dictated by the speed of a laboring locomotive on a curving switch track. Instead of setting the stacks parallel or at right angles to the tracks, they were " placed at an angle of twenty-two degrees, allowing a 200-foot radius for the entering switch." By such careful computations it was sought to avoid the moment wasted, to save the smallest fraction of a degree of heat which must otherwise be regained. So much for transporting metal. But a workman who lives a mile away from the mill gate has needlessly to criss-cross the checker-board streets of the town, for a distance easily calculable by the old formula that the square of the hypothenuse of a right-angled triangle is equal to the sum of the squares of the other two sides.

Our general failure to bring city planning to bear where it will count for most — that is, in zones of new construction — was personified in this instance by those Middle Western officials of the Steel Corporation who, as members of the Commercial Club of Chicago, were at this time contributing from their own pockets toward the $100,000 fund raised to work out in map and design the present magnificent city plan for Chicago, in which the genius of Daniel H. Burnham had its final expression. Yet as company officials they had

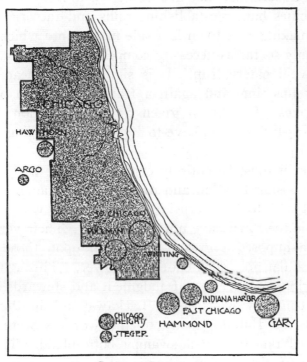

CHICAGO SATELLITES

not thought to secure the services of an expert city planner to lay out a brand-new town which, including the plant, involved an investment of over seventy-five million dollars. The Chicago city plan calls for a cutting of diagonal streets through old territory at enormous expense; the Gary town plan is likely to create in a decade conditions which can only be remedied by a similar Cæsarean operation.

The contention is raised, however, by some industrial leaders that they are in the business not of building cities but of establishing mills and factories, that the making of a town is a side matter into which they go only so far as necessity compels them. They want to avoid paternalism. It is significant to hear from their lips time and again a frank recognition of the mistakes of Pullman given as a justification for a " do-as-little-as-you-have-to " policy in shaping town conditions.

Yet it must be entirely evident that the early stage of choosing location and of laying the framework of plant and town is crucial. The citizens who are to people the town have not yet arrived. Their very absence imposes a greater obligation upon those with whose fiat goes such enormous power. Through such a serious miscarriage of judgment and stewardship by the company which built Lackawanna,[1] in the outskirts of Buffalo, many of the workers were long housed on stilts in a swampy bottomland. The efforts of the present administration to overcome the situation in so far as is now possible illustrate the slow recognition (by a corporation which has learned through experience) that efficiency hangs on health

[1] See article by John A. Fitch in The Survey for October 7, 1911.

and human well-being and that a mill town in a swamp is as misplaced as a garden patch on a slag pile.

A manufacturing concern which makes highly finished cardboard products recently moved from the center of a large city to its outskirts, stating as one reason for the change that the smoky atmosphere prevalent in

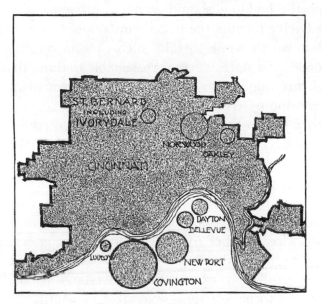

CINCINNATI SATELLITES

the city center caused great damage to the goods. Yet the effect of the same atmosphere on human lungs seemed to have been scarcely thought of. It was merely one of the fortunate coincidences of providence that what was good for keeping stock clean happened also to be good for the health of the workers.

The scientific thoroughness which would follow the

technique of efficiency and health down to the details of street planning is illustrated by the drawings for the construction of a large state prison by the Westinghouse, Church, Kerr Company. The firm went to the length of studying astronomical observations to determine the exact angle of the compass at which the building should stand in order to secure in each twelve months the maximum amount of sunlight. If it is worth while to take such care in housing the prisoners of a state, it seems reasonable to think that the same care might also be expended on street plans and the housing of free city dwellers.

How far we have yet to go in these directions in guiding development with reference to the community as a whole is illustrated by the fact that even at Flint — where a few years ago public-spirited citizens secured a well-known city planner to lay out a scheme for parks, boulevards and other civic features — one section after another of the industrial quarter was laid out adjacent to the automobile plants " without any special regulation except the understanding that no street was to be less than sixty feet in width." Fairfield is an example of a planned mill suburb. It seems extraordinary that we do not require in the case of every new subdivision — just as we require of every new tenement house — a careful plan on lines broadly laid down by public authority and submitted to it for approval. The Washington (state) proposal that one-tenth of the area of every such subdivision must be set aside for parks and playgrounds is a step in the right direction. To safeguard the future in old towns as well as new, such broad legislation as is found in the English Town Planning Act is essential in this country.

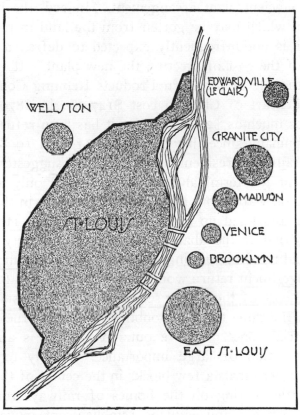

EDWARDSVILLE (LE CLAIR)

WELLSTON

GRANITE CITY

MADISON

ST·LOUIS

VENICE

BROOKLYN

EAST ST·LOUIS

ST. LOUIS SATELLITES

From an economic standpoint, employer and employee — the plant and the home — are differently affected by the suburban movement.

Removal from the city center, where land values have greatly risen, to the outskirts where land is not so valuable, often means to the manufacturer other gains besides plenty of space in which to secure the most efficient plant arrangement. Indeed, the higher return which may be gotten from the land in the city center is not infrequently expected to defray a large part of the cost of erecting the new plant. It is said that the site of the Corn Products Refining Company in the heart of Chicago cost $147,000 in 1879, and that as much as $2,500,000 for it has been refused by the company since they moved to Argo in 1908.

A railroad president in Chicago has suggested that some of the terminal stations be moved only a few blocks outward from their present locations in the city center and lined up together on one street. He estimates that if the abandoned trackage property were devoted to office buildings and other business purposes, the investment return would be sufficient to pay for the entire cost of the whole series of great new stations. Much the same thing is doubtless generally true when industrial concerns move out. Yet there is another consideration of large importance. Merely to shift railway terminals a few blocks in the center of the city has little bearing on the homes of railway workers. But when a manufacturing establishment moves out into a specially prepared suburb, the cheap land soon begins to rise rapidly in value as workingmen's homes begin to cover it. The question now arises whether this increase of land values accrues to the company,

to the householders, or — as in the English Letchworth — to the community.

A pamphlet which was distributed by the Pullman
Company at their World's Columbian Exposition exhibit in 1893 contains the statement that "the day is
not only coming, but is near at hand, when the $30,-
000,000 present capital stock of the Pullman Company
will be covered by the value of the 3,500 acres of land
on which is built the town of Pullman." That this
harvest was being reaped may be suspected from the
fact that the company did not relinquish the business
of owning and renting real estate until the supreme
court of Illinois ordered it so to do on the ground that
the company's charter did not authorize it to engage
in such business.

Some of the smaller mill towns, especially in the
South, suffer through the persistence of this policy
along with other almost feudalistic company powers.
But the present developments in establishing satellite
cities show less of an inclination on the part of those
who create them to monopolize the land and its increase in value.

Indeed, there is to-day quite as much danger from
the opposite tendency. The "let alone" policy not
only allows such matters as city planning to go by de-
fault, but sometimes throws into the hands of specu-
lating real-estate promoters the land values which inevitably come with community growth.

In Gary the land company, subsidiary of the Steel
Corporation, explains that in the subdivision which it

developed, the purpose has been to sell land and houses to employees at prices scarcely more than the original cost of the land plus improvements and interest charges. In the few years of Gary's existence, the land company has only once advanced the price of lots and houses. This presents a pleasing contrast with the booming operations of some real-estate speculators to be found in other subdivisions of Gary and in the general run of satellite cities.

Yet home ownership, which such a policy promotes, may often be a very doubtful advantage to the workingman. The land value created by the community is dependent upon the permanency of the community, and this is dependent upon the existence, stability and

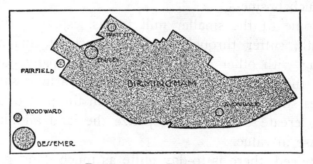

BIRMINGHAM SATELLITES

growth of the industrial plant. In a large city if one plant runs slack or is abandoned, there is likelihood of compensating growth in another plant. In the satellite city, as in a mushroom mining town, the home-owner is often at the mercy of the vicissitudes of a single industry.

To illustrate: Cherry is an isolated Illinois prairie town surrounding a mine shaft. Everything in the place depends upon this one source of wages. Before the disaster of 1909 many of the thriftiest men had put their savings into homes. Had it not been for relief funds their widows would soon have had to move where they could get work to support their families. The homes would very likely have been sold at only a small fraction of the amount invested in them. When, too, a mine town is suddenly abandoned because the company finds that the vein is exhausted or can no longer be profitably worked, the same loss of investment in homes occurs. The small manufacturing community dependent upon one concern may as suddenly become a deserted village if an invention displaces the product manufactured, or if an industrial combination is formed and decides to discontinue the local plant.

This risk in home ownership lurks in some degree in almost every satellite city. A safeguard, however, has been provided in Gary. The contract of sale between the Gary Land Company and the workingman purchasing real estate gives him the opportunity at any time of selling the house back to the company for the same amount which he paid for it, less a sum — to cover interest, depreciation, etc.— totaling little more than what rent for the period would have been. As a matter of fact, the home-owner in the steel company's subdivision can, as things stand to-day, sell out at a substantial profit to outsiders who are desirous of securing homes. The housing accommodations in Gary thus far are inadequate, and the interurban service brings in many workmen who live elsewhere. A considerable number even make the trip from Pullman to Gary and back each day, a distance of over twelve miles.

Transportation is a many-sided factor in the industrial suburb. It may tend to reduce the risk in home ownership if houses can be conveniently occupied by people who work in near-by towns. It may also broaden the opportunity for work, already discussed, for it may relieve the local industry from being the sole dependence.

Transportation facilities between large cities and their industrial suburbs vary widely. Sugar Creek lies a mile and a half beyond the end of the nearest Kansas City street-car line. But traction service of at least average quality connects South Omaha with Omaha, and Norwood with Cincinnati. Not a few of the workers in the packing plants in South Omaha live in Omaha proper, since they can easily reach their work on the street car. A publishing house which moved its plant out of New York to a beautiful location near the Hudson River, found that most of its employees did not change their residence, but continued to live in New York, and commute out into the country and back each day. A similar situation exists at Norwood and Oakley, near Cincinnati. The failure of work-people to move their homes out to the neighborhood of the plant may in some cases be due to high land prices set by the owners of real estate.   Or perhaps other members of the same family work " downtown," and so the family continues to live in the congested center.   Desire of youth to be near the amusements, the lights and the crowds — where " something is doing " all the time — is another factor.

Metropolitan advantages, it may be noted in passing, have attractions for the better-to-do also.   Margaret F. Byington has pointed out,[1] in discussing the influence of transportation upon the social life of Homestead, twenty-six miles up the Monongahela, that it is both too good and not good enough.   It is so good that the Homestead people who earn the largest incomes and have the shortest hours are able to go to Pittsburgh for concerts, entertainments and social gatherings.   Yet it is not good enough and cheap enough to enable the rank and file, who have least to spend and work long hours, to have the same advantages.   Meanwhile, because of the proximity to Pittsburgh, no local interest is shown by the very people who would otherwise tend to establish the general recreational facilities of a town of 25,000, and who might lead the social and civic life of the place.

Recreation and social life may need quite as much, if not more, wholesome opportunity and promotion in the industrial suburb, with its isolation and its sudden massing of strangers, as in the city center with its longer established neighborhoods and its greater fa-

[1] *See* "Homestead: The Households of a Mill Town," a volume in the Pittsburgh Survey, by Margaret F. Byington.

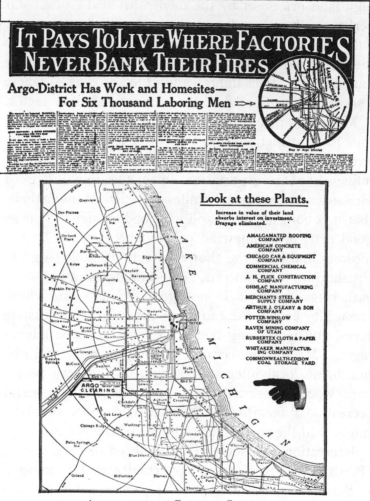

ADVERTISING A CHICAGO SATELLITE

   The full-page display in a Chicago newspaper above pointed out
"a golden opportunity for the builder or building operator." At
the bottom of the page a picture of a crowded trolley car, with men
sitting on the roof, illustrated " workmen coming from miles around
because the demand for flats and houses is greater than the supply."

cilities. Schools, libraries and similar civic institutions are criteria by which to gauge the standard of community life. Adequate provision for them may be of business value to the suburban plant management in keeping people contented away from the city. On the other hand, like camp sutlers, the traffickers in demoralization are quick to follow the trail of the satellite cities. A saloon-keeper who is making large profits at one of the most advantageous locations in Gary was shrewd enough to discern a similar chance at Argo, where his name is to be found over the door of the first established and principal saloon in the place.

One of the most serious industrial and community issues created by the isolation of satellite communities is bound up in the natural desire of the plant control to have always at hand a work force large enough to completely man the plant when running at its greatest producing capacity, a force large enough to carry the maximum work load. There can be no doubt that employers appreciate fully that home ownership tends to anchor the workman in the community. Rare is the plant that is always working at its greatest producing capacity. If the variation is comparatively slight, it may be handled by temporarily drawing upon the large surplus of labor which is usually to be found floating around the big city near-by. If, however, the extent to which the plant is worked varies all the way from 30 per cent. capacity up to the maximum, a grave problem confronts the population

which endeavors to make its home in the industrial
suburb.

Intermittent employment cannot comfortably be accompanied by intermittent meals. Housing must be
continuous even if employment is not. If the community has many establishments representing diversified industries, lack of work may not involve all at the
same time. Moreover, work-people temporarily laid
off at one factory often have an opportunity to earn
something elsewhere until their regular trade offers
them a job. In the satellite city dependent on a single
industry or plant, this opportunity is in a large
measure lacking.

To meet this condition some such industrial establishments run part-time or use in construction work
employees who are temporarily not needed in certain
departments. Desire to tide the workers over the
slack times may be prominent in the mind of the plant
manager, and for this he should have credit. But
fully as strong a motive must lie in the desire to have
experienced workers readily available when the plant
starts up. This sort of management tends, of course,
to discourage the worker from seeking elsewhere a
steadier job at his trade. There may be some compensating social values in keeping the worker in one
place instead of roving around, but the family strain
and social cost are heavy.

According to the general secretary of the Associated
Charities of Omaha the average family handled by the
branch office at South Omaha is less hopeful and

harder to put on its feet than the average family handled in Omaha proper. An inquiry at the South Omaha branch office revealed the fact that intermittent work has much to do with this. The wage-earner may have been idle three days this week, a day and a half last week, not at all the week before, and two days the week before that. Such irregularity in work breeds irregularity in habits of living. The community offered scarcely anything to occupy slack time except saloons in which to loaf. Intemperance, immorality and general shiftlessness were said to be more prevalent and deep-seated in these South Omaha poverty-stricken families than in similar families in Omaha.

Home ownership and arrangement of part-time work are not the only factors which are sometimes counted upon to control the currents in an industrial community. Some company officials act on the belief that by removing workingmen from a large city it is possible to get them away from the influences which foment discontent and labor disturbances. The satellite city is looked to as a sort of isolation hospital for the cure of chronic "trouble."

In an eastern city which recently experienced the throes of a turbulent street-car strike, the superintendent of a large industrial establishment frankly said that every time the strikers paraded past his plant a veritable fever seemed to spread among the employees in all his work-rooms. He thought that if the plants were moved out to the suburbs, the workingmen would

24

not be so frequently inoculated with infection. The experiences of Pullman in 1894 and Lawrence in 1912 are, of course, against this conclusion; but the question remains an interesting one to explore; how far does the removal of work-people from the big centers of population undermine the strength of trade unions.

It is equally important to know whether, in these towns of their own creation, the industrial interests seek to dominate the local government. Will people assert themselves as citizens when their interest runs counter to those to whom they, as workers, look for a livelihood? On the other hand, in these towns the industrial power can be more clearly singled out than in the complex metropolitan center, and Professor Ely, in making a study of Pullman in 1885 — but four years after the town's beginning — found that already a feeling had arisen that it was a praiseworthy thing to " beat the company."

At Gary one feels that friction and antagonism between townspeople and the industrial control are always just under the surface if not cropping out. The town of Steger, where pianos of that name are manufactured, recently had a controversy of the most acrimonious sort between the firm and citizens who charged despotic exploitation of the kind alleged at Pullman. At Leclaire, the town founded by the firm of N. O. Nelson, relations seem to have been harmonious. The elections of socialistic mayors in Granite City and Flint are to be weighed against elections at

Gary, whereby six saloon-keepers became members of a board of nine aldermen.

The politics of the satellite city have a bearing also on the large center near which it is located. Its vote, for example, might turn the tide of the whole district of which it is a part for or against the candidates who represent the newer policies for assuring popular control of government. More important still, many industrial suburbs will probably be absorbed sooner or later as sections of the metropolitan city. Pullman, for example, may be said to have completed a cycle upon which later industrial suburbs are only now starting. It has for several years been a part of the city of Chicago. Just what has Pullman contributed to the greater city? Does its town plan fit in with the great city plan recently formulated for the metropolitan district? What peculiar problems, if any, does it inject — of health, housing, recreation — into the well-being of the whole city? What sort of aldermen come from Pullman to the city council? These and other phases of the present-day estate of this, the first and perhaps most widely known, industrial suburb, will be discussed in the next chapter.

The industrial exodus, in which Pullman early played the rôle now taken by Gary, is, in its individual parts, a consciously directed movement. It therefore presents repeated opportunities for shaping the civic and social conditions under which large groups of working people are to live for decades to come. It raises in new and searching ways questions as to the obligations which go with economic control, as to the future of local self-government in relation to that control, and as to the organization and large-scale civic development of our industrial districts.

Like the foundlings which were dropped in the turn-cradles of the old-time orphanages, these young communities which industry is leaving at the doorsteps of our cities are no longer things apart and by themselves. For better or worse, they come to share in the common lot.

CHAPTER II

REDISCOVERING AN EMPLOYER'S UTOPIA

PULLMAN! The word teems with suggestion. For those who early hailed the town as providing that crucible in which the labor problem was to be transmuted by Utopian paternalism, the mention of the name brings memories as of a dream which vanished under the impact of reality. For "practical" men it signifies the futility of social betterment schemes and marks the battleground where law and order triumphed over anarchy — in the struggle of 1894 which, before it ended, embraced the transportation service of the country and saw the rise and fall of the American Railway Union under Eugene V. Debs. But for the host of warm-hearted, sane believers in the better day that is coming, it stands for a great human tragedy, yet a necessary one in so far as it made of paternalism a "lost cause."

In the perspective of the years we can understand the aspiration and the disappointment of the strong man whose hopes and plans for a model industrial community were shattered even in the hour of his victory over his own men. And we can sympathize with the men who, having grievances at least in some degree just, went through the hard struggle to bitter defeat, yet in that hour knew not that their fight had sealed the fate of paternalism and left open but one road — the road toward industrial democracy.

Our concern in the Pullman of to-day is to find out what heritage — industrial, civic and social — the past has turned over to the present and the future. What bearing has the history of this first well-known satellite city upon the problems of those which industry is creating to-day? " The Story of Pullman " distributed at the Pullman exhibit at the World's Columbian Exposition, Chicago, 1893, declared that " At an early date the beautiful town of Pullman . . . will be as a bright and radiant little island in the midst of the great tumultuous sea of Chicago's population; a restful oasis in the wearying brick-and-mortar waste of an enormous city."

To-day, twenty-two years later, it would seem worth while to re-discover this little " island " and see what it means in the sea of Chicago's life — in health, recreation, housing, and community spirit. Has Chicago been led to better dwellings by the model town? What of the provisions for wholesome play under paternalism and under public auspices? What of the people themselves who live in Pullman? Does the industry continue to supply the old houses with dwellers? Have strange people come in who know nothing of the ancient glories of their habitation? What of work conditions to-day as compared with those of twenty years ago? We now ride in steel instead of

wooden cars; how does this affect the workmen who
fashion them? Does our greater safety and comfort
mean greater or less skill on their part? Did they
find themselves, at the change, with useless trades on
their hands? What significance is there in the fact
that the first Socialist who ever sat as alderman in
Chicago's city council came from the ward of which
Pullman is a part, came indeed from a work-bench in
the Pullman car shops?

The old Pullman was the subject of countless radiant descriptions. The whole country watched the
dream of its founder take form. In 1880 open
prairie stretched westward from Lake Calumet,
broken only by the small farming community of Roseland. Five years later, when the chiefs and commissioners of the various state labor bureaus visited the
new town, they found the great car works surrounded
by nearly nine thousand dwellers in 1,520 houses having 6,485 rooms. Every house and tenement was
supplied with water and gas. The streets were wide,
well built and clean, lined with beautiful lawns and
trees, all cared for by the company. A complete system of drainage had been installed before the population came.

From the railroad station, fourteen miles from
downtown Chicago, a broad boulevard, now 111th
Street, led eastward to Lake Calumet. North of this
boulevard were the great shops, a park and artificial
lake forming an attractive landscape between them and
the railway station. South of the boulevard and visi-

ble from the station were the hotel, the Arcade —
containing stores, bank, theater and library — a park
with gardens and a bandstand, and beyond it the
Green Stone Church, the whole making a " civic center " which would do credit even to our modern town
planning.   A block south was the school building.

PULLMAN IN THE EARLY DAYS

Arcade Park, the Green Stone Church and the better houses

Beyond this grouping of the more imposing buildings were a dozen city blocks of dwellings with a conveniently located market building.   The nearer blocks
contained the better houses, in solid rows, yet with
some diversity of architecture, while the further
blocks were given over to the cheaper tenement buildings which presented a monotonous similarity of ex-

teriors and of interior arrangement. More blocks of dwellings occupied the tract immediately north of the shops. At the Lake Calumet terminus of the boulevard was a small island. Here the recreation field was laid out, and games of all sorts were encouraged. Crack cricket matches and the most famous rowing regattas of the Middle West shared with baseball and bicycle races in bringing renown to the place as an athletic center.

But beneath this attractive picture of the "model town" was the spirit and substance of paternalism. A cardinal point in the policy of the president of the Pullman Company was the retention of the ownership of land and houses. Maintenance of utilities, care of houses and lawns, repair and cleaning of streets, management of hotel, theater and other community activities — all were controlled by the company. Thus was established that autocratic power, which scarcely was challenged until 1885, when Professor Richard T. Ely assailed it as feudalistic.

It is easy to criticize an autocrat, but even the social worker, who sometimes turns his imagination to the things he would do if he were mayor of a city or president of an industrial concern, little knows how subtly his own conviction as to "what is good for people" might estrange him from them when they failed to share the conviction. It is not hard to understand the jealous guidance Mr. Pullman sought to exercise over the activities of the town he so fondly created. The evident sincerity of his benevolent intentions

blinded most of the early observers to the real significance of such enormous power over private affairs
of life, and their descriptions consisted of unmixed
praise.

In characterizing the president of the Pullman Company as " the modern *King Lear,*" Miss Addams, in
her paper written just after the strike, showed how
the honest desire to give his employees the best surroundings developed into a sense of pride and power
in his own benevolence, how " he cultivated the great
and noble impulses of the benefactor until the power
of attaining a simple human relationship with his employees was gone from him." The story of Pullman,
so far as its significance for to-day is concerned, centers largely in the developments whereby the feudalistic power was dislodged and shifted to the shoulders
of the community. The annexation of Pullman to
Chicago in 1889 was the beginning. The vigor with
which the company opposed this step indicated a real-
izing sense that it foreshadowed the end of company
control of the town.

The great strike was the next important factor in
the disintegration of that control. The trouble centered in a situation involving fixed rents and sliding
wage scales, both controlled by the company. The
latter suffered in the general business depression following the World's Fair. It claims to have accepted
contracts at a loss in order to continue to afford work.
But it cut its wage scales 22 per cent. and reduced its
schedules of working time. The men struck.

In the midst of the struggle a sympathetic strike was ordered by the new American Railway Union whose members crippled the railway service of the country by their refusal to handle Pullman cars. The action of President Cleveland in sending federal troops to Chicago started a bitter controversy in which the governor of Illinois and local officials claimed that their control of the situation was adequate and that the President's action was unwarranted. The imprisonment of Eugene V. Debs, president of the American Railway Union, gave added sting to the defeat of the organization by the railway managers and undoubtedly helped to give Debs his leadership of the Socialist party.

The sympathetic strike and its attendant violence was widely condemned — the railroad brotherhoods, for example, refusing to take part in it. But the original and more orderly strike of the Pullman employees was based upon grievances in some measure just, in the estimation of nearly every investigator, from the government commission, headed by Carroll D. Wright, to an attorney for one of the railroads later involved, who is now identified with one of our largest industrial corporations. It was this strike that demonstrated how unsatisfactory the domination of community interests by the industrial authority could be if the form were kept up without the loyalty of both parties.

The third great event in the waning of this domination was the Illinois Supreme Court decision in 1898 to the effect that the charter of the Pullman Company did not permit it to hold real estate beyond the necessities of its manufacturing business. Five years were allowed for disposing of these holdings, and at the end of that period an extension of five years was granted. By 1908, therefore, the local possessions of the company were reduced to little more than the car shops. However, the remaining vacant land was retained by much the same interests. The Pullman Land Association was the agent by which this was accomplished, and of the 4,000 acres originally purchased, approximately 2,900 are still owned by this association. The shops occupy about 500 acres, and some 600 acres were sold. Hotel, market building, school, church — all passed out of the company's hands. To retain some remnant of the cherished project of her husband, Mrs. Pullman purchased the Arcade, which she still owns.

Growth of population and civic development are daily enhancing the value of the 2,900 acres of vacant land still held by the Pullman Land Association. This is probably the largest single holding of vacant land in Chicago. As pointed out previously [1] the increase of value anticipated by the company was by no means small. The price paid in 1880 is said to have averaged about $200 an acre. A real-estate man estimates it to be worth now at least $1,500 an acre. The association is selling portions from time to time for development as residential subdivisions.

[1] Page 15.

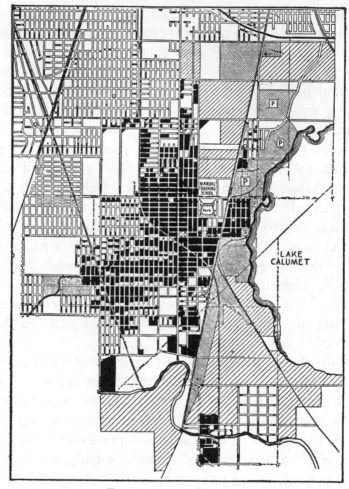

PULLMAN AND VICINITY

 Territory built up.

Areas used for industrial purposes. P indicates land
occupied by Pullman Car shops.
Vacant land still owned by Pullman Land Association —
2,900 acres out of 4,000 bought in 1880, one of the
largest single holdings of vacant land in Chicago.

The change from company ownership and management of real estate and community institutions to that of individuals and the public has meant a distinct gain in many respects. This is especially to be seen in provision of school and recreation facilities and healthier community relationships. But nevertheless the old town is left with a forlorn air of faded glory. The city of Chicago does not maintain the streets so well, and out of sheer regard for the immediate surroundings of the shops, the company still assumes the maintenance of 111th Street, the boulevard, and the thoroughfare along the western front. The old lawns which made each street beautiful in the old days are kept up or not, as the present owners happen to elect, and often adjoining premises show a glaring contrast. Hard, bare ground in front of the tenement blocks permits their ugly monotony to stand out to-day in all its nakedness, a monotony previously softened by the flanking greensward and hedges. These block houses, unsuitable for sale to the occupants of their tenements, were bought by Mr. Pullman's daughter, Mrs. Frank O. Lowden. Her agent rents them under the supervision of the same caretaker, or " house boss " as he is called, who has been employed since the beginning.

Except for these block houses and some of the cheaper rows of dwellings north of the shops, which are held by the Pullman Land Association, the houses of the town were offered to the occupants at prices averaging one hundred times the monthly rental. Easy terms of payment were arranged, on installments scarcely larger than rent, and some purchasers are still paying off the few remaining installments. The number of employees who thus became owners of the houses which they and their families had come to call homes was gratifying to those whose hearts clung to the high hope in which the town was founded. Individual effort due to pride in home ownership has brightened the Pullman of to-day with an after-glow reflecting the earlier beauty. A Saturday afternoon stroll shows many a householder working to improve his own dwelling.

The substantial original construction of brick and the architectural scheme still give the houses of Pullman a distinct stamp in contrast with the stretches of dingy, frame houses characteristic of Chicago's poorer sections. They appear like a transplanted fragment of one of our eastern cities. Chicago housing seems not to have been influenced in the slightest degree by the "model" on its outskirts. While Chicago has only recently come up to the tenement light and air standards set up by Pullman thirty years ago, that progress seems part of the country-wide advance.

The block houses which contain the bulk of the cheapest tenements show the lowest conditions of living in the town of Pullman.

They are occupied to-day almost exclusively by Poles, Hungarians, Italians and Greeks. Seven of these houses south of the shops contain 246 apartments: 36 of two rooms, 88 of three rooms, 98 of four rooms and 24 of five rooms. The rents vary from $5 a month for two rooms to $8 for four rooms, while some of the five-room tenements are $10. Although rents in general have risen, those at Pullman show very little actual change from the rates of thirty years ago. Then Pullman rents were considerably higher than tenement rents in Chicago, or in Massachusetts manufacturing towns, as the report of the labor commissioners showed. The accommodations were much superior, however. Now, for accommodations of even poorer grade in Chicago a rate of at least a third more must be paid.

Sanitary conditions are not as bad as one usually finds in the cheaper of Chicago tenements. Each room has one or more windows giving adequate light and air. Practically none opens on a narrow court. A bath-tub is a rarity, which seems strange in a "model town," but it must be remembered that the standards of 1880 were not those of to-day. Occasional overhaulings of plumbing and sanitary conveniences in the block houses have kept them in a fair state of repair, though there is considerable complaint concerning dilapidation of sinks and odors from them, and renovation of walls might be more frequent. The .scrubbing of hall floors is undertaken by the rather unusual method of apportioning the space equally among the families whose tenements are entered through the hall.

Crowding is doubtless more serious than formerly, though statistics for the earlier days are difficult to find. The "house boss" of the block houses estimated in 1913, that about 1,600 people lived in the 848 rooms of the 246 tenements above mentioned. This is an average of about six to a tenement and nearly two to a room. But a relief visitor considered even this estimate of crowding as conservative, because of the secretiveness of the families as to the number of their boarders. One case, for example, was cited of a husband and wife, eight children and two boarders — all in a tenement of two rooms. Not infrequently a large group of single men, usually Greeks, inhabits a tenement. That the problem of the boarder, however, is not a new one is indicated by a description of the town written in 1893 by the wife of an official. At that time it appeared that no fewer than nine hundred families in Pullman had one or more boarders or roomers, and that from 2,500 to 3,000 " bachelors " worked at Pullman. The work force at that time numbered less than 7,000.

This crowding cannot fail to be a menace, especially since the tenements in the block houses have little privacy with respect. to toilet arrangements. The three tenements on each floor of an entry-way have their closets grouped at one end of the common hall.

To accommodate more people in a given space, some of the smaller houses seem to have gone through an evolution from single to two-family dwellings. For example, a whole block of exactly similar houses north of the shops, each formerly containing five rooms and renting for $12, is now divided, so that each contains a two-room tenement downstairs, and a three-room

The "Block Houses"

Alley Entrance Tenements

Contrast in Home Owner's Care

HOUSING AT PULLMAN

41

tenement upstairs, each renting for about $6.50.
The appearance of the houses from the street remains
unchanged, but the only entrance to the upstairs tenements is through the rear alley and thence up a flight
of wooden stairs from the back yard.

South European immigration displacing earlier
comers from the North is responsible in some measure
for the crowding and for many other changed conditions in the town. The influx of new nationalities is
shown most strikingly by a comparison of the working
force of 1893 with that of 1913. The number of
American-born decreased slightly, but those of North
European nativity decreased from 66 to 33 per cent.
of the total, while those born in Central and Southern
Europe increased from 6 to 43 per cent. of the total.
The table on page 43 shows this comparison by countries of birth.

The extent of the change which has come about in
twenty years is vividly shown by the fact that within
one week after the opening of the hostilities between
Turkey and the Balkan States, no fewer than two
hundred out of an estimated five hundred Greeks in
Pullman and the surrounding district started back to
join the army of their fatherland.

The flood of foreigners from Southern Europe to
America has been coincident with many changes in
industrial processes, lessening the premium upon skill.
Pullman affords spectacular proof of this. The ad-
vent of the steel car threw wood-carving, cabinet-
making and many other skilled crafts on the scrap

	1893	Per Cent.		1913	Per Cent.
Americans		1,346	28		3,432	24
North Europeans						
Scandinavian ..	1,072			2,007		
British	898			1,099		
German	620			959		
Dutch	573	3,163	66	683	4,748	33
Central and South Europeans						
Austro-Hungarian	83			2,313		
Russian and Lithuanian ..	10			1,187		
Italian	75			1,110		
Polish	92			1,099		
Greek	1	261	6	228	5,937	43
		4,770			14,117	

heap and substituted metal work demanding distinctly
shorter training. Steel sleepers were first made about
1907. This year not a single one of wood is being
manufactured. Of the ordinary coaches built on contract for railroads, about 75 per cent. are steel body
and wooden interior finish, 15 per cent. are all steel,
and only 10 per cent. are of wood. More would probably be made entirely of steel but for the difficulty experienced in heating them while in service.

The plant consists of three principal divisions: the

passenger-car construction shops, employing about 68 per cent. of the total work force; the repair shops employing about 10 per cent., and the freight-car shops employing about 22 per cent. In 1885 Professor Ely found that the great majority were skilled artisans and that the unskilled constituted about one-quarter of the force. To-day the force may be classified into 50 per cent. skilled, 26 per cent. semi-skilled, and 24 per cent. unskilled. The proportion of unskilled and semi-skilled would be still greater were it not for the introduction of many labor-saving devices.

When the steel construction began all the older and skilled employees were encouraged to learn the newer trades and officials say that many of the cabinet-makers readily adapted themselves to the changed conditions, utilizing much of their old skill in the steel cabinet work. But they frankly admit that the great amount of semi-skilled work such as the assembling, erecting and riveting of steel cars has borne hard on the older employees who cannot " stand the racket." Slavs, who " don't seem to have any nerves," take these jobs. What this means for the older employees was vividly pointed out by a Dutch tradesman in Roseland who said that when the steel-car work came in about two hundred members of the Dutch church he attended left, saying that the change of trades was too much for them and that anyway " no white man would now want to work in some departments of the shops."

Nevertheless, the company officials are able to show a proud record as to the average length of service of

their employees. Those who have served less than
two years are for the greater part unskilled " floaters."
The remainder — between two-thirds and three-
fourths of the whole — have served over two years
and make up the permanent force with an average
service of no less than twelve years. In 1906 the
number who had served twenty years or more was
641. To-day it is estimated at over one thousand.
A considerable number of employees started as young
men of twenty to thirty when the shops were built in
1880, and are therefore men of about sixty now.

While the experience of these men includes the
great strike of 1894, and company officials claim that
most of the strikers came back, the other side of the
picture is shown by a " broken and discouraged man "
representing a superior type of the English working
class — one of the strike leaders — who stood before
Miss Addams three years afterward. " Although he
had been out of work most of the time since the
strike," she says in " Twenty Years at Hull House,"
" he had been undisturbed for six months in the repair
shops of a street-car company, under an assumed
name, but had then been discovered and dismissed,"
believing that he was so blacklisted that his skill could
never be used again.

The average wage is nearly 30 cents an hour. The
lowest rate paid is 20 cents an hour, to unskilled day
labor. The average for semi-skilled labor is 24 to
26 cents an hour for work by the day, but much more
than this for piece work in the erecting and riveting

departments. Mechanics earn generally 40 or 50 cents an hour. It will be noted that the rate for un-skilled labor compares favorably with the 17½ cents an hour paid by the Steel Corporation at South Chicago and Gary. There is a fifty-four-hour week in all departments — 9¾ hours a day, except Satur-day when the shops close the year round at 12:15, as against the ten- and twelve-hour days, and until re-cently the seven-day week, of the steel workers.[1]

Wage rates signify little, however, unless yearly earnings are computed from the time books. The company claims that work is steady, that in general fluctuations are not matters of weeks and days, but that at various times the orders of railroads for cars drop seriously, as they did in 1910. The only peri-odic slack season is one of six weeks each summer in the repair shops, the surplus workers being used in the construction shops. But the freight-car shops, using mainly semi-skilled and unskilled labor, are most often affected by intermittency of employment. Tested by different years the industry would seem to have rather serious ups and downs. In 1905, for instance, the number of employees went nearly as low as 1,100; in early 1910 it was almost up to 15,000; in 1912 it was about 10,000; while in 1913 it went up, as the fore-going table shows, to over 14,000.

What becomes of the "casuals"? Many of them are wandering workmen who rarely stay long in one

[1] These statistics of wages and hours are based on data for the year 1913.

place, even with steady work, but are off to some spot
of real or fancied advantage.   Others are immigrants.
But many, doubtless, native and foreign alike, " stay
put "— especially if they own their homes — and
worry along over periods of unemployment or seek
other work in the vicinity to fill in.   " Very irregular "
work is given by the Chicago United Charities as one
of the causes of poverty among Pullman work-people.
A man of good habits can usually get credit to tide
him over the periods of unemployment.   " It takes,
however, a large part of the wages of the regular
season to pay up these bills, so a decent standard of
living is often impossible."   Typical applicants for relief are :

1. Young man, support of old parents, laid off for
three months.   Bills accumulating and assistance asked.

2. Italian with wife and five children.   Only irregular
employment.   Grocer had cut off credit, landlord press
ing for rent.   School principal reports children in need
of shoes.

3. Dutch family.   Father had been employed in shops
twenty years, laid off for three months.   Wife and six
children.

Diversity of industries in near-by plants provides
against unemployment when the main industry runs
slack.   The report of the state labor commissioners
in 1884 shows that even at that early date Mr. Pullman was seeking to assure greater industrial stability
to his town by encouraging other manufacturing con-

cerns to settle near-by. To-day, the Sherwin-Williams Paint Company, the Chicago Drop Forge and Foundry Company, the Griffin Car Wheel Company, and other concerns are grouped just south of Pullman; the Illinois Central railroad shops are just to the north; the West Pullman factory district includes a plant of the International Harvester Company; and street or interurban cars reach many other large plants in the general region.

The labor policy of the Pullman Company is conservative. While many of its employees are trade-union members, the organizations are in no way recognized, but an "open shop" practice prevails. There is little indication of any more liberal attitude toward collective bargaining than that indicated in the reply of Vice-President Wickes nearly twenty years ago when President Cleveland's commission to investigate the Pullman strike asked if it were not inevitable that with the company's great power its representatives, in bargaining ability, were always far superior to the individual workman. " Yes, that's his misfortune," said he. Yet the question whether the fifty-four-hour week should be divided into six days of 9 hours each or into five of 9¾ hours, leaving Saturday as a 5¼-hour day was submitted to a vote of the men, who chose the latter arrangement. But one wonders how far the company would go in submitting questions which mean more to it than the alternative between six or half a dozen. The company's conservatism is indicated by its electing not to come under the provisions of the

Illinois Workmen's Compensation law. Yet its policy in payment of damages to injured workmen is said to be increasing in liberality. Relief for illness or injury incurred while on or off duty is granted in meritorious cases, but there is no definite plan, although one is in contemplation.

A pension system was adopted by the company January 1, 1914. It is administered by a board composed of company officers and is entirely voluntary on the part of the company. It is modeled on the general lines adopted by other large industrial and railroad companies, but is said to be more liberal than the majority. Male employees at seventy years of age and female employees at sixty-five are entitled, after twenty years of service, to a pension of 1 per cent. per year of service, based on the average monthly pay received during the last full year of employment. The minimum pension is $15 a month and there is no maximum limit.

Attention is also being directed to welfare work. The activity of one stockholder roused the company to an effort in preventing occupational diseases.[1] It had been needlessly killing men by lead poisoning in the paint shops and by dangerous acids, fumes and dust-laden air in other departments. The success of the preventive efforts is shown by the fact that in July, 1911, there were 77 cases of lead poisoning out of 450 men employed in the paint department, while in

[1] See "What One Stockholder Did," *The Survey,* June 1, 1912.

August, 1912, not a single case was reported among
470 employed. Five doctors now care for injuries as
compared with one formerly. Thus far no nurse has
been employed, although a nurse's services, especially
among the single men living in lodgings, would go
far to prevent infections due to the improper care of
minor wounds.

Community agitation and action brought about the
elimination of a serious menace to life — the grade
crossing of the Illinois Central and Michigan Central tracks, half a block from the main entrance to the
Pullman works. Across the tracks, in Roseland,
Kensington and other neighborhoods, live the majority
of Pullman employees. Counting the interurbans,
from 200 to 300 trains rushed over this crossing every
day. Two through trains passed at top speed within
a few moments of 5.30 P. M., quitting time for 9,000
men. The coroner's records for a recent period of
twenty-two months show forty-one deaths on railroad crossings in Pullman and vicinity. A disclosure
of the situation by a local newspaper, coupled with
vigorous activities on the part of the South End Business Men's Association and various improvement associations, stirred the whole community. A committee of fifty citizens induced the Chicago City Council
to pass an ordinance requiring the elevation of the
tracks before December 31, 1916.

Decent housing was not the only means by which
the company sought at the beginning to provide wholesome home surroundings. Effort was also made to

ward off demoralizing influences. With the exception of the bar in the Florence Hotel, no saloons were allowed in the town. Liquor interests seized upon the nearest available spot and thirty grog shops soon clustered at Kensington just across the railroad tracks and south of Pullman. This place quickly merited

MODERN SHOPS AT PULLMAN

Dangerous grade crossing near main gate, now eliminated by track elevation. In a recent period of twenty-two months, forty-one deaths occurred on grade crossings near the Pullman works.

the name of "Bumtown," which still clings to it. Even until recently the last suburban train each night from the city down to Kensington and return was known as " the Bumtown turn-around."

With the changes in population and the property sale which did away with the early restrictions, saloons seem strangely slow in invading the old town. Aside from the hotel bar mentioned only five saloons have started up, one of them in a corner of the market house. And in the part of the town north of the shops but ten have come in. In fact few things are more striking to the observer who watches the swarms of men at the main gate during the noon hour than the absence of beer cans and the prevalence of milk bottles. From two milk wagons as many as five hundred bottles of milk are sold at noon, and the number in very warm weather rises still higher. Kensington in 1912, however, still had fifty-two saloons, twenty-five of which were on the single block nearest to Pullman. Several prohibition districts, however, are stoutly maintained in Roseland and vicinity under the local option law. This law accounts in part for the absence of saloons in Pullman proper. It requires the consent of the majority of frontage ownership and of householders in any block before a saloon license may be issued.

The police administration of the district has not had at all times the highest respect of the better citizens. Indeed a scandal which came to the attention of all Chicago occurred in connection with an indecent entertainment to celebrate the presentation of a diamond star to the police lieutenant by a group of citizens of the sort usually interested more in the non-enforcement than in the enforcement of law. But the region seems to be generally law-abiding. An officer of the Juvenile Protective Association declared that although there were some " blind pigs " in the doubtful shacks along Lake Calumet and a few bad dance halls in Kensington, the neighborhood was the cleanest she had ever worked in. She found, however, evidence, particularly in Burnside, of a condition which social observers are increasingly noting in our industrial communities — loose relations in houses where a group of Slavic men have one woman as housekeeper.

The company management of the town sought to provide various wholesome substitutes for the demoralizing influences which were barred. Through the generosity of Mrs. Pullman the library, already mentioned, is still maintained, and its present circulation of books, greater now than formerly, is noteworthy in the face of the incoming Slavic, Greek and Italian population and the fact that it has no books in these languages. It is used mainly by children. The theater is now little used. Its location up one flight of stairs conflicts with Chicago's building requirements. And the people of Roseland, which has outstripped Pullman in size, prefer to patronize their own motion-picture and vaudeville theaters.

Recreation facilities show one of the most significant developments in the change from the old paternalistic régime to the newer public control. The island athletic field was a notably serviceable provision, but its glory is eclipsed by the splendid recreation center, Palmer Park, which the South Park commissioners admirably placed so as to serve Pullman on the east, Kensington on the south and Roseland on the west.

Its forty acres provide football and baseball fields, tennis courts, swimming pool, children's playground and wading pool, outdoor and indoor gymnasiums for both sexes, club-rooms and an assembly hall for social gatherings and entertainments. The fine civic service of these Chicago recreation centers has often been described.[1]

This service not only supplies the neighborhood with splendid facilities for recreation and social gatherings but stimulates community coöperation and a spirit of neighborliness. It is worth noting that Palmer Park serves as a frequent meeting place for the district representatives of the Juvenile Protective Association, the United Charities and the Visiting Nurses' Association and that in all the efforts for neighborhood welfare which center at the park the school principals are enthusiastic coöperators. It is a pity that the same cannot be said of all the clergy. Although the churches are probably larger and better attended than in the average city neighborhood, they have in general taken little share in movements for community betterment.

Schools no less than recreation facilities serve to give assurance that public authority can go paternalism one better in meeting community needs. It is not fair, of course, to contrast the fine new George M. Pullman grade school which the Chicago Board of Education has built, with the discarded and forlorn building across the street, which marks the remains of a

[1] See article in The Survey for July 2, 1910.

Palmer Park Recreation Center

The New George M. Pullman Public School

MODERN MUNICIPAL PROVISION FOR COMMUNITY NEEDS

glory now dim.   But the school built by the company
is declared by school authorities not to have been up
to the highest standards of its time.   And it is particularly pointed out that to have placed it where it would
be a part of the showy front of the town as seen from
the railroad was not the best from the standpoint of
its efficiency as a school.   When Pullman became a
part of Chicago the Board of Education might have
bought the building, but the company would not sell.
When the property was disposed of in accordance with
the court order the board refused to buy, but continued
to rent until it built the new school.   Six other schools,
including a high school, serve the region around Pullman, and three of the principals have twenty years or
more of service to their credit.

The community is at last supplied with the Pullman Free Manual Training School for which Mr.
Pullman's will in 1897 provided $1,200,000.   This
fund increased to well over $2,000,000.   While it
has been contended that delay was necessary in order
that the sum should become large enough to carry out
the project most effectively, the trustees have been
taken to task by a local newspaper, which also sought
to show by the estimate of an accountant that the fund
should by this time have reached nearly $3,000,000.
A head for the school was selected in Professor L. G.
Weld, formerly of Iowa State University.   The insti-
tution occupies a most convenient and appropriate site
of forty acres just north of and facing Palmer Park.

The health conditions of Pullman and its vicinity

seem to be fully up to and perhaps better than those of the average city neighborhood, though among the children of the poor in the block houses and other cheap tenements the work of an infant welfare nurse from the Chicago Department of Health finds plenty of scope. The most pressing immediate needs are for sewage disposal and hospital service. The sewerage system empties, through the Calumet River, into Lake Michigan, which supplies the city's water. Accordingly a canal is now being provided which will connect with the main Chicago sanitary canal and thus divert all sewage to the Mississippi.

The problem of hospital service is one which affects the whole southern portion of Chicago. Mr. Pullman, for some unknown reason, failed to include a hospital in his elaborate scheme of buildings. There are private hospitals at the Illinois Steel Works in South Chicago and at the Illinois Central Railroad shops at Burnside. Public-spirited citizens organized a small hospital in Pullman, which receives patients from the car shops as well as from the town in general. But the charity patient, whether for a clinic or the county hospital, must make the long journey into the central part of the big city. A fifteen-mile journey — by Kensington police ambulance to the Illinois Central suburban train, thence in the baggage car to downtown Chicago, and thence by another police ambulance to the county hospital — is certainly not conducive to a sick man's recovery. Instances are not lacking of deaths en route. Within a year a change has been

affected whereby county hospital patients are taken
all the way by motor ambulance. But tuberculosis
dispensary patients still have the train journey to take.
The situation will be remedied when a branch of the
county hospital is built, for which land has already
been bought at Burnside just north of Pullman.

The growth of the neighborhoods west of Pullman
directs attention to the problem of city planning.
While the number of people living in the old town
of Pullman is nearly the same as it was twenty-five
years ago, Roseland, Kensington, West Pullman and
Gano have all developed from rural communities until,
according to the 1910 census, the population table
shows:

Roseland 20,901
Pullman 7,931
Kensington 6,328
West Pullman 6,025
Gano 4,660

The history of these towns is interesting. Roseland was settled by a group of Hollanders who left
the old country in 1849 because of religious difficulties.
Preaching services in Dutch are still held in three
churches. Gano, just west of Kensington and south
of Roseland, contains many French Canadians, who
are said to have come originally about 1885 to act as
strike-breakers during a strike at the brickyards. The
Catholic church they founded has French preaching
services on alternate Sundays.

The development of the section seems to have been along natural lines of traffic.   From the standpoint of the Chicago city plan no peculiar problems are apparent either in this newly built-up region or in the old arrangement of Pullman.   The general district is following the usual course of an outlying portion of the city.   Real-estate operators are developing it by subdivisions.   This means more or less haphazard growth, with attention focused on the profits to be derived out of given plots rather than upon the development of the whole area in accordance with modern scientific town planning.

Interest in city planning seems to be absorbed in industrial, and particularly harbor, development rather than in residential growth.   The utilization of Lake Calumet for harbor purposes was part of the original Pullman scheme.   But in these later days the enterprise affects not only the industries of the Pullman vicinity but the whole of Chicago.   With a direct channel leading from the Calumet River to Lake Calumet, the dredging of the latter, and the construction in it of huge docks, the metropolitan harbor facilities would be greatly increased in a way to relieve congestion nearer the city center.   One of the tentative schemes includes not only the harbor development, but a much needed diagonal avenue from Pullman and vicinity to South Chicago, another boulevard connecting with the Chicago boulevard system, and a park to be made possible by a filling-in of the northern part of Lake Calumet.   The location of the park is criticized because the suggested docks would shut it off from the Lake Calumet waterfront. A park along the wooded banks of the Calumet River to the south is also proposed. Both lake and river shores are suggested park areas in the Chicago city plan. The city is now negotiating with shore owners for the release of their riparian rights.

The civic spirit of the people shows strongly the influence of their experiences with industrial authority. Even in 1885 Professor Ely found difficulty in getting real opinions on living and working conditions from the dwellers in the town who feared " spotters " and dire consequences if they criticized the company. " To beat the company " was already considered praiseworthy. But the bitterness generated by the strike is of course in considerable measure explanatory of prior and subsequent feeling.

While the company declares that the men were free to live where they chose, there is little dispute that it felt compelled to give preference in the shops to company tenants. In antebellum days the sturdy Dutchmen who had founded the neighboring village of Roseland made it one of the important stations of the " underground railroad " from the Ohio River to Canada. Lively stories are told of how Constable Kuyper played the genial host to the man-hunters who were searching for runaway slaves stowed in his own chimney. A similar spirit of independence was shown by not a few Pullman employees who chose to live in the freer air of Roseland rather than be sure of a job

under the wings of paternalism.   And when the Pullman Company finally relinquished its ownership of
Pullman the trend to Roseland continued.

In little ways the old suspicion and submerged bitterness continues to crop out.   It is related that some
of those who were interested in planning the projected
manual training school fell into conversation with a
Pullman workman who did not know with whom he
was talking.   They at once sought to test the enthusiasm of the workers for the new technical opportunities which would soon be available.   But they are
said to have been discomfited by a reply to the effect
that " we have sweated our years away in those shops
and if possible we'll keep our boys from slaving their
lives out in them too."

Whatever there may have been in the incident is not
so important in itself as in its expression of some
measure of sentiment, however unrepresentative of the
whole.   The prevalence of a similar feeling among
the boys themselves with reference to working in the
shops is vouched for by a man whose position brings
him into intimate contact with them.   And the temper
of the community is indicated in some degree by the
fact that a fair-minded and influential citizen was quite
willing to believe the report — which the company
contends is utterly false — that after a well-paid old
German had become expert in giving steel-car fittings
a " graining " to resemble mahogany the company put
some young fellows alongside to learn the secret of
his skill and then discharged him.

But the politics of the community afford perhaps the most significant sidelights on civic spirit and the feeling toward the Pullman Company. One of the struggles of the early days is related by the late William T. Stead in his book, " If Christ Came to Chicago." John P. Hopkins, as a young man, held a good position with the company but showed both his independence and usefulness to such an extent that although he was discharged for insubordination the company later reëmployed him. Then, although Mr. Pullman was a pronounced Republican, Hopkins proceeded to carry the town for the Democratic ticket, his popularity among the voters being due, it is said, to admiration for his standing unabashed and victorious before the company. This was too much and he was discharged without ceremony. By the turn of political fortune he was the mayor of Chicago at the time of the Pullman strike.

The extent to which the company has sought to dominate the politics of the community is a matter on which opinions vary. Probably efforts in this direction were much more in evidence formerly than now. At the time of Professor Ely's study, the village of Hyde Park — of which Pullman was then a part — had as town clerk and as treasurer officers of the Pullman Company. With one exception every member of the local board of education was an officer of the Pullman Company or its allied concerns. But no resident of Pullman, who was not an officer of the company, had any public office.

One of the aldermen from the ward of which Pullman is a part, recently declared that an officer of the
Pullman bank frankly told him that he thought the
company ought to have representation and influence in
local politics especially with reference to police administration. But as a matter of fact the suspicion
that any aldermanic candidate is " in " with the company is enough to make his defeat certain. This has
actually happened three times — upon two occasions a
former Pullman shop manager going down to disaster. A study of the election returns from the various
precincts during a period of years shows a greater
anti-company strength among men of independent
mind who moved over to Roseland than among the
more docile dwellers in Pullman.

The ward is known as a " banner ward " among the
Socialists who normally poll from 12 to 18 per
cent. of the vote. Neither Socialists nor their op-
ponents say that this strength of their party is due directly to the strike of 1894, or to personal loyalty to
the leader of the sympathetic strike, Eugene V. Debs.
But there can be no doubt that the events of that
tragic summer did much to give many men the frame
of mind which made them easy converts to the Socialist party, and the Socialist handbills one can see pasted
on the inside walls of the car shops indicate Socialist
strength and zeal among the Pullman employees.

It seems reasonably clear, however, contrary to the
conclusion to which the average man would naturally
jump, that the election in this ward of the first Social-

ist alderman who ever sat in the Chicago City Council had little relation to any feeling generated by the strike a few years before. The Democratic candidate was manifestly unfit and the Municipal Voters' League indorsed the Republican. A few days before the election the League learned of the Republican's dubious past and issued a special bulletin advocating the election of the Socialist. Although the ward was normally Republican, its voters showed remarkable independence by electing the Socialist, who was a workman in the Pullman shops. He turned out to be a hopelessly incompetent, though entirely honest and sincere, alderman. It is interesting to speculate, however, what might have happened in Chicago's later politics if he had been a man of the strenuous ability of Victor L. Berger.

The independent voting thus shown is characteristic of the ward. Later when two Republican aldermen seemed to become less efficient and devoted in their public service, it promptly elected two Democrats. These rendered efficient service, according to the estimate of the Municipal Voters' League. Both of the repudiated aldermen had voted for doubtful franchises. Even the better of them voted to grant twenty-year rights to a street-car company whose rights had still nine years to run. Under the terms of the new franchise there was a continuance of the old ten-cent fare — recently reduced to five cents — for the ride from Pullman into Chicago's downtown section. During these same tenures of office, more-

over, a so-called "bargain" was made whereby the
Pullman Company agreed that if the city of Chicago
would collect the garbage and refuse from Pullman
it might dump the same in Lake Calumet along the
company's riparian rights.   Thus considerable land
was "made"— illegally, according to an Illinois legislative commission.

A better alderman who followed fought not only
against this so-called "grab," but against the filling-in
of more land in Lake Calumet by manufacturing concerns just south of the Pullman shops.   He furthermore stopped these concerns from building a fence
across a street which had been open to the public for
thirty-eight years.   In 1913 a Progressive was elected
in place of one of the Democrats.   The former Pullman shop manager ran a bad fourth.   So it has come
about that thirty years from the founding of this
feudal industrial town a citizenship has developed
which can scarcely be matched elsewhere in Chicago
for vigorous independence in standing out against en-
croachment upon community rights by industrial interests.

The development of Pullman shows the foresight
of a pioneer mind.   Mr. Pullman early recognized the
advantages of the removal of industry to the suburbs
and saw the strategic possibilities of a Calumet harbor.   He secured much land while yet it was cheap,
and realized the economies of wholesale town and
house building.   And he provided recreation and tenements far in advance of the times, setting standards

which Chicago failed to follow until years later, when hard struggle secured tenement laws and the movement for playground and recreation centers became successful.

But, as we have seen, the break-up of the model scheme came through failure to reckon with the human element. The collective land values and other advantages of collective ownership were originally sought for the benefit of the company and not for the community. The company ownership of housing was not flexible. Nor would individual home ownership have been sufficiently flexible under the stress of industrial changes which have so affected the make-up of the working force. There was no effort to devise a newer or more pliant plan. We have seen this neglect of the human side illustrated again in the failure to provide a hospital and adequate protection against industrial diseases.

Throughout the twenty years following the early clash between paternalist and striker, Pullman has had a new equilibrium. Inside the plant, the company has been in control. Like monopoly prices, kept down by potential competition, its power over the work day is limited only by the potential bargaining ability of the workers and not by their actual collective voice. But this autocracy which remains in control of the newer field of industry could not extend to the community life where citizenship is reënforced by the long traditions of Anglo-Saxon democracy. The experience at Pullman has shown that while the men have not been able to dictate to the company as to work, the company has not been able to dictate to the men as to life.

One thus returns with mingled impressions from a voyage to re-discover Pullman. The melancholy reminders of a past, which had much that was worthy but which was swept away with the inrush of a newer spirit, cannot fail to appeal to the emotions. But the big feeling is one of faith in the movement of American democracy, which found at Pullman a turning-point significant in ways we may yet only dimly appreciate. William T. Stead lamented over the fact that Marshall Field, Philip D. Armour and George M. Pullman — Chicago's big business triumvirate of that day, " each supremely successful in his own respective lines, each superbly generous and liberal in the matter of private benefaction "— failed to utilize their remarkable talents in promoting the efficiency and service of Chicago as a municipality.

To-day, as one sees at Pullman the people providing for their own needs — splendidly as in the case of the schools and recreation center, imperfectly as in such administrative matters as street maintenance, gropingly as in the one-sided efforts toward city planning — and sees the instinctive righteousness and good judgment of the " plain folks " as revealed in political action, one finds a firmer assurance that through the genius not alone of great men but rather of America's common life the way lies toward a better civilization.

CHAPTER III

A MODERN LEAR

A Parenthetical Chapter By
JANE ADDAMS

This analysis of paternalism was written in 1894 immediately after the great Pullman strike. It was not published at the time because of its personal nature, although much of the material, omitting the Lear analogy, was used later in "Democracy and Social Ethics." Miss Addams interprets forces which were at the height of their power twenty years ago. As brought out in the preceding chapter, only the shell of this employer's Utopia remains, and the town is part of Chicago. But the problem which she thus dramatizes reasserts itself to-day in the conflict between corporation control and community life throughout many of our newer industrial districts.

THOSE of us who lived in Chicago during the summer of 1894 were confronted by a drama which epitomized and, at the same time, challenged the code of social ethics under which we live, for a quick series of unusual events had dispelled the good nature which in happier times envelops the ugliness of the industrial situation. It sometimes seems as if the shocking experiences of that summer, the barbaric instinct to kill, roused on both sides, the sharp division into class lines, with the resultant distrust and bitterness, can only be endured if we learn from it all a great ethical lesson. To endure is all we can hope for. It is impossible to justify such a course of rage and riot in a civilized community to whom the methods of conciliation and control were open. Every public-spirited citizen in Chicago during that summer felt the stress and perplexity of the situation and asked himself, " How far am I responsible for this social disorder? What can be done to prevent such outrageous manifestations of ill-will? "

If the responsibility of tolerance lies with those of the widest vision, it behooves us to consider this great social disaster, not alone in its legal aspect nor in its sociological bearings, but from those deep human motives, which, after all, determine events.

During the discussions which followed the Pullman strike, the defenders of the situation were broadly divided between the people pleading for individual benevolence and those insisting upon social righteousness; between those who held that the philanthropy of the president of the Pullman Company had been most ungratefully received and those who maintained that the situation was the inevitable outcome of the social consciousness developing among working people.

In the midst of these discussions the writer found her mind dwelling upon a comparison which modified and softened all her judgments. Her attention was

caught by the similarity of ingratitude suffered by an
indulgent employer and an indulgent parent. *King
Lear* came often to her mind. We have all shared
the family relationship and our code of ethics concerning it is somewhat settled. We also bear a part
in the industrial relationship, but our ethics concerning that are still uncertain. A comparative study of
these two relationships presents an advantage, in that
it enables us to consider the situation from the known
experience toward the unknown. The minds of all
of us reach back to our early struggles, as we emerged
from the state of self-willed childhood to a recognition of the family claim.

We have all had glimpses of what it might be to
blaspheme against family ties; to ignore the elemental
claim they make upon us, but on the whole we have
recognized them, and it does not occur to us to throw
them over. The industrial claim is so difficult; the
ties are so intangible that we are constantly ignoring
them and shirking the duties which they impose. It
will probably be easier to treat of the tragedy of the
Pullman strike as if it were already long past when
we compare it to the family tragedy of *Lear* which
has already become historic to our minds and which
we discuss without personal feeling.

Historically considered, the relation of *Lear* to his
children was archaic and barbaric, holding in it merely
the beginnings of a family life, since developed. We
may in later years learn to look back upon the industrial relationships in which we are now placed as quite

as incomprehensible and selfish, quite as barbaric and undeveloped, as was the family relationship between *Lear* and his daughters. We may then take the relationship of this unusually generous employer at Pullman to his own townful of employees as at least a fair one, because so exceptionally liberal in many of its aspects. *King Lear* doubtless held the same notion of a father's duty that was held by the other fathers of his time; but he alone was a king and had kingdoms to bestow upon his children. He was unique, therefore, in the magnitude of his indulgence, and in the magnitude of the disaster which followed it. The sense of duty held by the president of the Pullman Company doubtless represents the ideal in the minds of the best of the present employers as to their obligations toward their employees, but he projected this ideal more magnificently than the others. He alone gave his men so model a town, such perfect surroundings. The magnitude of his indulgence and failure corresponded and we are forced to challenge the ideal itself: the same ideal which, more or less clearly defined, is floating in the minds of all philanthropic employers.

This older tragedy implied maladjustment between individuals; the forces of the tragedy were personal and passionate. This modern tragedy in its inception is a maladjustment between two large bodies of men, an employing company and a mass of employees. It deals not with personal relationship, but with industrial relationships.

Owing, however, to the unusual part played in it

by the will of one man, we find that it closely approaches *Lear* in motif. The relation of the British King to his family is very like the relation of the president of the Pullman Company to his town; the dénouement of a daughter's break with her father suggests the break of the employees with their benefactor. If we call one an example of the domestic tragedy, the other of the industrial tragedy, it is possible to make them illuminate each other.

It is easy to discover striking points of similarity in the tragedies of the royal father and the philanthropic president of the Pullman Company. The like quality of ingratitude they both suffered is at once apparent. It may be said that the ingratitude which *Lear* received was poignant and bitter to him in proportion as he recalled the extraordinary benefits he had heaped upon his daughters, and that he found his fate harder to bear because he had so far exceeded the measure of a father's duty, as he himself says. What, then, would be the bitterness of a man who had heaped extraordinary benefits upon those toward whom he had no duty recognized by common consent; who had not only exceeded the righteousness of the employer, but who had worked out original and striking methods for lavishing goodness and generosity? More than that, the president had been almost persecuted for this goodness by the more utilitarian members of his company and had at one time imperiled his business reputation for the sake of the benefactions to his town, and he had thus reached the height of sacrifice for it.

This model town embodied not only his hopes and ambitions, but stood for the peculiar effort which a man makes for that which is misunderstood.[1]

It is easy to see that although the heart of *Lear* was cut by ingratitude and by misfortune, it was cut deepest of all by the public pity of his people, in that they should remember him no longer as a king and benefactor, but as a defeated man who had blundered through oversoftness. So the heart of the Chicago man was cut by the unparalleled publicity which brought him to the minds of thousands as a type of oppression and injustice, and to many others as an example of the evil of an irregulated sympathy for the " lower classes." He who had been dined and fêted throughout Europe as the creator of a model town, as the friend and benefactor of workingmen, was now execrated by workingmen throughout the entire country. He had not only been good to those who were now basely ungrateful to him, but he felt himself deserted by the admiration of his people.

In shops such as those at Pullman, indeed, in all manufacturing affairs since the industrial revolution, industry is organized into a vast social operation. The shops are managed, however, not for the development of the workman thus socialized, but for the interests of the company owning the capital. The divergence between the social form and the individual aim be-

---

[1] While the town of Pullman was in process of construction the Pullman stock was sometimes called out on the New York Exchange: "How much for flower-beds and fountains?"—to which the company naturally objected.

comes greater as the employees are more highly
socialized and dependent, just as the clash in a family
is more vital in proportion to the development and
closeness of the family tie. The president of the
Pullman Company went further than the usual employer does. He socialized not only the factory but
the form in which his workmen were living. He
built and, in a great measure, regulated an entire town.
This again might have worked out into a successful
associated effort, if he had had in view the sole good
of the inhabitants thus socialized, if he had called upon
them for self-expression and had made the town a
growth and manifestation of their wants and needs.
But, unfortunately, the end to be obtained became ultimately commercial and not social, having in view the
payment to the company of at least 4 per cent. on
the money invested, so that with this rigid requirement there could be no adaptation of rent to wages,
much less to needs. The rents became statical and the
wages competitive, shifting inevitably with the demands of trade. The president assumed that he himself knew the needs of his men, and so far from wish-
ing them to express their needs he denied to them the
simple rights of trade organization, which would have
been, of course, the merest preliminary to an attempt
at associated expression. If we may take the dicta-
torial relation of *Lear* to *Cordelia* as a typical and most
dramatic example of the distinctively family tragedy,
one will asserting its authority through all the entangle-
ment of wounded affection, and insisting upon its sel-

fish ends at all costs, may we not consider the absolute
authority of this employer over his town as a typical
and dramatic example of the industrial tragedy? One
will directing the energies of many others, without regard to their desires, and having in view in the last
analysis only commercial results?

It shocks our ideal of family life that a man should
fail to know his daughter's heart because she awk-
wardly expressed her love, that he should refuse to
comfort and advise her through all difference of opinion and clashing of will. That a man should be so
absorbed in his own indignation as to fail to apprehend
his child's thought; that he should lose his affection in
his anger, is really no more unnatural than that the
man who spent a million of dollars on a swamp to
make it sanitary for his employees, should refuse to
speak to them for ten minutes, whether they were in
the right or wrong; or that a man who had given them
his time and thought for twenty years should with-
draw from them his guidance when he believed them
misled by ill-advisers and wandering in a mental fog;
or that he should grow hard and angry when they
needed tenderness and help.

Lear ignored the common ancestry of *Cordelia* and
himself. He forgot her royal inheritance of magna-
nimity, and also the power of obstinacy which he
shared with her. So long had he thought of himself
as the noble and indulgent father that he had lost the
faculty by which he might perceive himself in the
wrong. Even when his spirit was broken by the storm

he declared himself more sinned against than sinning. He could believe any amount of kindness and goodness of himself, but could imagine no fidelity on the part of *Cordelia* unless she gave him the sign he demanded.

The president of the Pullman Company doubtless began to build his town from an honest desire to give his employees the best surroundings. As it developed it became a source of pride and an exponent of power, that he cared most for when it gave him a glow of benevolence. Gradually, what the outside world thought of it became of importance to him and he ceased to measure its usefulness by the standard of the men's needs. The theater was complete in equipment and beautiful in design, but too costly for a troupe who depended upon the patronage of mechanics, as the church was too expensive to be rented continuously. We can imagine the founder of the town slowly darkening his glints of memory and forgetting the common stock of experience which he held with his men. He cultivated the great and noble impulses of the benefactor, until the power of attaining a simple human relationship with his employees, that of frank equality with them, was gone from him. He, too, lost the faculty of affectionate interpretation, and demanded a sign. He and his employees had no mutual interest in a common cause.

Was not the grotesque situation of the royal father and the philanthropic employer to perform so many good deeds that they lost the power of recognizing

good in beneficiaries? Were not both so absorbed in
carrying out a personal plan of improvement that they
failed to catch the great moral lesson which their times
offered them? This is the crucial point of the tragedies and may be further elucidated.

Lear had doubtless swung a bauble before *Cordelia's*
baby eyes that he might have the pleasure of seeing
the little pink and tender hands stretched for it. A
few years later, he had given jewels to the young prin-
cess, and felt an exquisite pleasure when she stood
before him, delighted with her gaud and grateful to
her father. He demanded the same kind of response
for his gift of the kingdom, but the gratitude must be
larger and more carefully expressed, as befitted such
a gift. At the opening of the drama he sat upon his
throne ready for this enjoyment, but instead of delight
and gratitude he found the first dawn of character.
His daughter made the awkward attempt of an un-
trained soul to be honest, to be scrupulous in the expressions of its feelings. It was new to him that his
child should be moved by a principle outside of himself, which even his imagination could not follow;
that she had caught the notion of an existence so vast
that her relationship as a daughter was but part of
it.

Perhaps her suitors, the *King of France* or the *Duke
of Burgundy,* had first hinted to the young *Cordelia*
that there was a fuller life beyond the seas. Certain
it is that someone had shaken her from the quiet measure of her insular existence and that she had at last

felt the thrill of the world's life.   She was transformed
by a dignity which recast her speech and made it
self-contained, as is becoming a citizen of the world.
She found herself in the sweep of a notion of justice
so large that the immediate loss of a kingdom seemed
of little consequence to her.   Even an act which might
be construed as disrespect to her father was justified
in her eyes because she was vainly striving to fill out
this larger conception of duty.

The test which comes sooner or later to many parents had come to *Lear,* to maintain the tenderness of
the relation between father and child, after that relation had become one between adults; to be contented
with the responses which this adult made to the family
claim, while, at the same time, she felt the tug upon
her emotions and faculties of the larger life, the life
which surrounds and completes the individual and
family life, and which shares and widens her attention.
He was not sufficiently wise to see that only that child
can fulfill the family claim in its sweetness and strength
who also fulfills the larger claim, that the adjustment
of the lesser and larger implies no conflict.   The mind
of *Lear* was not big enough for this test.   He failed
to see anything but the personal slight involved; the
ingratitude alone reached him.   It was impossible for
him to calmly watch his child developing beyond the
strength of his own mind and sympathy.

Without pressing the analogy too hard may we not
compare the indulgent relation of this employer to his
town to the relation which existed between *Lear* and

Cordelia? He fostered his employees for many years, gave them sanitary houses and beautiful parks, but in their extreme need, when they were struggling with the most difficult question which the times could present to them, when, if ever, they required the assistance of a trained mind and a comprehensive outlook, he lost his touch and had nothing wherewith to help them. He did not see the situation. He had been ignorant of their gropings toward justice. His conception of goodness for them had been cleanliness, decency of living, and above all, thrift and temperance. He had provided them means for all this; had gone further, and given them opportunities for enjoyment and comradeship. But he suddenly found his town in the sweep of a world-wide moral impulse. A movement had been going on about him and through the souls of his workingmen of which he had been unconscious. He had only heard of this movement by rumor. The men who consorted with him at his club and in his business had spoken but little of it, and when they had discussed it had contemptuously called it the "Labor Movement," headed by deadbeats and agitators. Of the force and power of this movement, of all the vitality within it, of that conception of duty which induces men to go without food and to see their wives and children suffer for the sake of securing better wages for fellow-workmen whom they have never seen, this president had dreamed absolutely nothing. But his town had at last become swept into this larger movement, so that the giving-up of comfortable homes, of beautiful surroundings, seemed as naught to the men within its grasp.

Outside the ken of this philanthropist, the proletariat had learned to say in many languages that " the injury of one is the concern of all." Their watchwords were brotherhood, sacrifice, the subordination of individual and trade interests to the good of the working class; and their persistent strivings were toward the ultimate freedom of that class from the conditions under which they now labor.

Compared to these watchwords the old ones which the philanthropic employer had given his town were negative and inadequate.

When this movement finally swept in his own town, or, to speak more fairly, when in their distress and perplexity his own employees appealed to the organized manifestation of this movement, they were quite sure that simply because they were workmen in distress they would not be deserted by it. This loyalty on the part of a widely ramified and well-organized union toward the workmen in a " scab shop," who had contributed nothing to its cause, was certainly a manifestation of moral power.

That the movement was ill-directed, that it was ill-timed and disastrous in results, that it stirred up and became confused in the minds of the public with the elements of riot and bloodshed, can never touch the fact that it started from an unselfish impulse.

In none of his utterances or correspondence did the president of the company for an instant recognize this

touch of nobility, although one would imagine that he
would gladly point out this bit of virtue, in what he
must have considered the moral ruin about him. He
stood throughout pleading for the individual virtues,
those which had distinguished the model workman of
his youth, those which had enabled him and so many
of his contemporaries to rise in life, when " rising in
life " was urged upon every promising boy as the goal
of his efforts. Of the new code of ethics he had caught
absolutely nothing. The morals he had taught his
men did not fail them in their hour of confusion.
They were self-controlled and destroyed no property.[1]
They were sober and exhibited no drunkenness, even
though obliged to hold their meetings in the saloon
hall of a neighboring town. They repaid their employer in kind, but he had given them no rule for the
higher fellowship and life of association into which
they were plunged.

The virtues of one generation are not sufficient for
the next, any more than the accumulations of knowledge possessed by one age are adequate to the needs
of another.

Of the virtues received from our fathers we can
afford to lose none. We accept as a precious trust
those principles and precepts which the race has worked
out for its highest safeguard and protection. But
merely to preserve those is not enough. A task is laid

[1] The bill presented to the city of Chicago by the Pullman Company for damages received during the strike was $26—the result
only of petty accidents.

upon each generation to enlarge their application, to ennoble their conception, and, above all, to apply and adapt them to the peculiar problems presented to it for solution.

The president of this company desired that his employees should possess the individual and family virtues, but did nothing to cherish in them those social virtues which his own age demanded. He rather substituted for that sense of responsibility to the community, a feeling of gratitude to himself, who had provided them with public buildings, and had laid out for them a simulacrum of public life.

Is it strange that when the genuine feeling of the age struck his town this belated and almost feudal virtue of personal gratitude fell before it?

Day after day during that horrible suspense, when the wires constantly reported the same message, " The president of the company holds that there is nothing to arbitrate," one longed to find out what was in the mind of this man, to unfold his ultimate motive. One concludes that he must have been sustained by the consciousness of being in the right. Only that could have held him against the great desire for fair play which swept over the country. Only the training which an arbitrary will receives by years of consulting first its own personal and commercial ends could have made it strong enough to withstand the demands for social adjustment. He felt himself right from the *commercial* standpoint, and could not see the situation from the *social* standpoint. For years he had gradually accustomed himself to the thought that his motive was beyond reproach; that his attitude to his town was always righteous and philanthropic. Habit held him persistent in this view of the case through all the changing conditions.

The diffused and subtle notion of dignity held by the modern philanthropist bears a curious analogy to the personal barbaric notion of dignity held by *Lear*. The man who persistently paced the seashore, while the interior of his country was racked with a strife which he alone might have arbitrated, lived out within himself the tragedy of "King Lear." The shock of disaster upon egotism is apt to produce self-pity. It is possible that his self-pity and loneliness may have been so great and absorbing as to completely shut out from his mind a compunction of derelict duty. He may have been unconscious that men were charging him with a shirking of the issue.

Lack of perception is the besetting danger of the egoist, from whatever cause his egoism arises and envelopes him. But, doubtless, philanthropists are more exposed to this danger than any other class of people within the community. Partly because their efforts are overestimated, as no standard of attainment has yet been established, and partly because they are the exponents of a large amount of altruistic feeling with which the community has become equipped and which has not yet found adequate expression, they are therefore easily idealized.

Long ago Hawthorne called our attention to the fact

that "philanthropy ruins, or is fearfully apt to ruin, the heart, the rich juices of which God never meant should be pressed violently out, and distilled into alcoholic liquor by an unnatural process; but it should render life sweet, bland and gently beneficent."

One might add to this observation that the muscles of this same heart may be stretched and strained until they lose the rhythm of the common heartbeat of the rest of the world.

Modern philanthropists need to remind themselves of the old definition of greatness: that it consists in the possession of the largest share of the common human qualities and experiences, not in the acquirements of peculiarities and excessive virtues. Popular opinion calls him the greatest of Americans who gathered to himself the largest amount of American experience, and who never forgot when he was in Washington how the " crackers " in Kentucky and the pioneers of Illinois thought and felt, striving to retain their thoughts and feelings, and to embody only the mighty will of the " common people." The danger of professionally attaining to the power of the righteous man, of yielding to the ambition for " doing good," compared to which the ambitions for political position, learning, or wealth are vulgar and commonplace, ramifies throughout our modern life, and is a constant and settled danger in philanthropy.

In so far as philanthropists are cut off from the influence of the *Zeit-Geist,* from the code of ethics which rules the body of men, from the great moral life spring-

ing from our common experiences, so long as they are
" good to people," rather than " with them," they are
bound to accomplish a large amount of harm. They
are outside of the influence of that great faith which
perennially springs up in the hearts of the people, and
re-creates the world.

In spite of the danger of overloading the tragedies
with moral reflections, a point ought to be made on the
other side. It is the weakness in the relation of the
employees to the employer, the fatal lack of generosity
in the attitude of workmen toward the company under
whose exactions they feel themselves wronged.

In reading the tragedy of " King Lear," *Cordelia*
does not escape our censure. Her first words are cold,
and we are shocked by her lack of tenderness. Why
should she ignore her father's need for indulgence, and
be so unwilling to give him what he so obviously
craved? We see in the old king " the overmastering
desire of being beloved, which is selfish, and yet characteristic of the selfishness of a loving and kindly nature alone." His eagerness produces in us a strange
pity for him, and we are impatient that his youngest
and best-beloved child cannot feel this, even in the
midst of her search for truth and her newly acquired
sense of a higher duty. It seems to us a narrow conception that would break thus abruptly with the past,
and would assume that her father had no part in her
new life. We want to remind her that " pity, memory
and faithfulness are natural ties," and surely as much
to be prized as is the development of her own soul.

We do not admire the *Cordelia* " who loves according to her bond " as we later admire the same *Cordelia* who comes back from France that she may include in her happiness and freer life the father whom she had deserted through her self-absorption. She is aroused to her affection through her pity, but when the floodgates are once open she acknowledges all. It sometimes seems as if only hardship and sorrow could arouse our tenderness, whether in our personal or social relations; that the king, the prosperous man, was the last to receive the justice which can come only through affectionate interpretation. We feel less pity for *Lear* on his throne than in the storm, although he is the same man, bound up in the same self-righteousness, and exhibiting the same lack of self-control.

As the vision of the life of Europe caught the sight and quickened the pulses of *Cordelia*, so a vision of the wider life has caught the sight of workingmen. After the vision has once been seen it is impossible to do aught but to press toward its fulfillment. We have all seen it. We are all practically agreed that the social passion of the age is directed toward the emancipation of the wage-worker; that a great accumulation of moral force is overmastering men and making for this emancipation as in another time it has made for the emancipation of the slave; that nothing will satisfy the aroused conscience of men short of the complete participation of the working classes in the spiritual, intellectual and material inheritance of the human race. But just as *Cordelia* failed to include her father in the

scope of her salvation and selfishly took it for herself
alone, so workingmen in the dawn of the vision are
inclined to claim it for themselves, putting out of their
thoughts the old relationships: and just as surely as
Cordelia's conscience developed in the new life and
later drove her back to her father, where she perished,
drawn into the cruelty and wrath which had now become objective and tragic, so the emancipation of working people will have to be inclusive of the employer
from the first or it will encounter many failures, cruel-
ties and reactions. It will result not in the position
of the repentant *Cordelia* but in that of *King Lear's*
two older daughters.

If the workingmen's narrow conception of emancipation were fully acted upon, they would hold much the
same relationship to their expropriated employer that
the two elder daughters held to their abdicated father.
When the kingdom was given to them they received
it as altogether their own, and were dominated by a
sense of possession; "it is ours not yours" was never
absent from their consciousness. When *Lear* ruled
the kingdom he had never been without this sense of
possession, although he expressed it in indulgence and
condescending kindness. His older daughters expressed it in cruelty, but the motive of father and children was not unlike. They did not wish to be reminded by the state and retinue of the old King that he
had been the former possessor. Finally, his mere
presence alone reminded them too much of that and
they banished him from the palace. That a newly ac-

quired sense of possession should result in the barbaric, the incredible scenes of bitterness and murder, which were *King Lear's* portion, is not without a reminder of the barbaric scenes in our political and industrial relationships, when the sense of possession, to obtain and to hold, is aroused on both sides. The scenes in Paris during the political revolution or the more familiar scenes at the mouths of the mines and the terminals of railways occur to all of us.

The doctrine of emancipation preached to the wage-workers alone runs an awful risk of being accepted for what it offers them, for the sake of the fleshpots, rather than for the human affection and social justice which it involves. This doctrine must be strong enough in its fusing power to touch those who think they lose, as well as those who think they gain. Only thus can it become the doctrine of a universal movement.

The new claim on the part of the toiling multitude, the new sense of responsibility on the part of the well-to-do, arise in reality from the same source. They are in fact the same " social compunction," and, in spite of their widely varying manifestations, logically converge into the same movement. Mazzini once preached, " the consent of men and your own conscience are two wings given you whereby you may rise to God." It is so easy for the good and powerful to think that they can rise by following the dictates of conscience by pursuing their own ideals, leaving those ideals unconnected with the consent of their fellow-men. The president of the Pullman Company thought out within his own mind a beautiful town. He had power with which to build this town, but he did not appeal to nor obtain the consent of the men who were living in it. The most unambitious reform, recognizing the necessity for this consent, makes for slow but sane and strenuous progress, while the most ambitious of social plans and experiments, ignoring this, is prone to the failure of the model town of Pullman.

The man who insists upon consent, who moves with the people, is bound to consult the feasible right as well as the absolute right. He is often obliged to attain only Mr. Lincoln's " best possible," and often have the sickening sense of compromising with his best convictions. He has to move along with those whom he rules toward a goal that neither he nor they see very clearly till they come to it. He has to discover what people really want, and then " provide the channels in which the growing moral force of their lives shall flow." What he does attain, however, is not the result of his individual striving, as a solitary mountain climber beyond the sight of the valley multitude, but it is underpinned and upheld by the sentiments and aspirations of many others. Progress has been slower perpendicularly, but incomparably greater because lateral.

He has not taught his contemporaries to climb mountains, but he has persuaded the villagers to move up a few feet higher. It is doubtful if personal ambition, whatever may have been its commercial results, has ever been of any value as a motive power in social reform. But whatever it may have done in the past, it is certainly too archaic to accomplish anything now. Our thoughts, at least for this generation, cannot be too much directed from mutual relationships and responsibilities. They will be warped, unless we look all men in the face, as if a community of interests lay between, unless we hold the mind open, to take strength and cheer from a hundred connections.

To touch to vibrating response the noble fiber in each man, to pull these many fibers, fragile, impalpable and constantly breaking, as they are, into one impulse, to develop that mere impulse through its feeble and tentative stages into action, is no easy task, but lateral progress is impossible without it.

If only a few families of the English-speaking race had profited by the dramatic failure of *Lear,* much heartbreaking and domestic friction might have been spared. Is it too much to hope that some of us will carefully consider this modern tragedy, if perchance it may contain a warning for the troublous times in which we live? By considering the dramatic failure of the liberal employer's plans for his employees we may possibly be spared useless industrial tragedies in the uncertain future which lies ahead of us.

CHAPTER IV

INDUSTRY'S ESCAPE FROM CONGESTION

THE suburbanite who leaves business behind at nightfall for the cool green rim of the city would think the world had gone topsy-turvy if at five-thirty he rushed out of a factory set in a landscape of open fields and wooded hillsides, scrambled for a seat in a street car or grimy train and clattered back to the region of brick and pavement, of soot and noise and jostle. Yet this is daily routine for many thousands of factory workers.

When industry moves out from the city center it is seeking economic advantage. It may provide also a made-to-order " model " town, or merely build rows of ' company houses," or leave housing to haphazard real-estate enterprise, or depend on traction to bring workers to the suburban shops. But its own purpose is always paramount — to escape from the handicaps of congestion and secure elbow-room, to establish an efficient modern plant where conditions are easy and land is cheap.

The " model town " is not the typical result of the movement of industry to the suburbs. Much more usual, if not so conspicuous, is the shifting of factories one by one to the edge of the city. The environs of

Cincinnati present unusual examples of this shift to escape congestion with industrial advantage the impelling motive, the workers continuing mainly to live in the crowded sections of Cincinnati.

The most widely known industrial plant on Cincinnati's outskirts is the soap factory of the Procter and Gamble Company. But Ivorydale, as the plant with its neighborhood is called, is chiefly noted for its profit-sharing schemes rather than the development of the community around it. Our interest is attracted by the recent and rapid industrial development of Norwood and Oakley which adjoin each other on the city's northeastern edge.

Starting as residential suburbs of the usual type, their shaded streets have been outflanked by a cordon of big factories stretching along the line of the Baltimore and Ohio Railroad. Most of these plants have emigrated from Cincinnati's center.

It was little more than ten years ago that a local chronicler hailed Norwood as " Gem of the Highlands, the brightest jewel in Cincinnati's sylvan crown." At a recent legislative hearing in Columbus she had become, in the words of her spokesman, " the Chicago of Hamilton County."

According to a federal census summary for 1909, Norwood boasted forty-nine manufacturing establishments capitalized at $13,368,000 with an annual product worth nearly $10,000,000. Among the larger plants are those of the Bullock Electric Works of the Allis-Chalmers Company which, in 1898, was the first

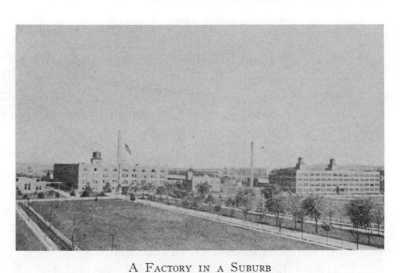

A FACTORY IN A SUBURB

United States Playing Card Company plant at Norwood. The
former plant was in downtown Cincinnati.

CITY TENEMENTS FOR WORKERS' HOMES

Nearly half the workers in the Norwood suburban factories live
in the crowded parts of Cincinnati.

to move out from Cincinnati; the United States Playing Card Company; the Weir Frog Company; and the
Globe-Wernicke Company which, in 1900, left its location in a crowded part of Cincinnati to reëstablish itself on twenty acres of cornfields.

Development in Oakley is yet more recent. In 1907
a "factory colony" seized upon land previously occupied by four dairies. These half-dozen plants not
only gained many individual advantages over their old
quarters in the congested city, but set up coöperative
additional ones to be used in common.

"Town booming" is the usual method by which
industries are brought to a new community. In the
case of Norwood, on the contrary, the factories en-
countered local indifference and even antagonism.
Many citizens feared that the residential character of
the place would be jeopardized. Real-estate men made
no effort to build houses and flats within the means of
factory workers; there was larger and surer profit in
residences for Cincinnati business men. The consequence is that, although a dozen years have elapsed
since the factories began to move out and although
Norwood has grown from 6,480 in 1900 to 16,185 in
1910, a comparatively small proportion of the operatives live in the vicinity of the factories. Rather,
suburbanites with business in Cincinnati have increased the Norwood population.

The actual living places of the Norwood and Oakley
wage-earners reveal a situation of peculiar interest to
the increasing number of civic experts who believe that

conditions should be changed so as to permit of people " walking to work." They hold that, with all our emphasis on the value of rapid transit as a means of lessening congestion, we must also approach the problem from the other side, and seek scientifically to reduce the need for traction through city planning which shall enable more people to live as neighbors to their means of livelihood.

Less than one-third of the operatives in Norwood and Oakley factories live within easy walking distance of their work. The great majority of those who must depend on traction facilities ride out from more or less congested parts of central Cincinnati. Some others even live in Kentucky, and thus, after journeying to and across the Ohio River, have then to traverse the city itself from boundary to boundary in order to reach their place of employment.

Data supplied by five of the larger Norwood factories and by the largest Oakley factory, covering nearly 4,500 workers, we may fairly assume to be representative of the total number of workers, about 10,000. The table and map on pages 96 and 97 indicate roughly where these workers live. Only those who live in Norwood and Oakley, and some of those in near-by neighborhoods, are within easy walking distance of the factories.

This dislocation of the normal routine of factory and home involves several problems. There is the need for travel and its curtailment of leisure and income; there are luncheons to be got by thousands of

HOMES OF NORWOOD AND OAKLEY EMPLOYEES:

Downtown Cincinnati

Per Cent.

West End, East End and other tenement and
crowded parts. Other parts near city's center 44.68

*Industrial Sections in Northwest Part of Cin-
cinnati*

Cumminsville, St. Bernard and other sections 6.00

Kentucky

Covington, Newport and scattering........ 4.96

Country Towns 5.95

Norwood and Oakley 31.28

Vicinity of Norwood and Oakley

Hyde Park, Madisonville, Evanston and other
neighborhoods both in and out of Cincinnati, some just inside and some just beyond
the Cincinnati city limits................. 7.13

_____

100.00

employees at a distance from home and the customary city facilities; there are less tangible effects on the
permanency of the working force and their isolation
from their fellows.

For the hauling of raw material and the shipping of
finished product, the Baltimore and Ohio Railroad offered the same freight rates as for Cincinnati. Shipping facilities were a large factor in the location of
plants at Norwood and Oakley. But the means for

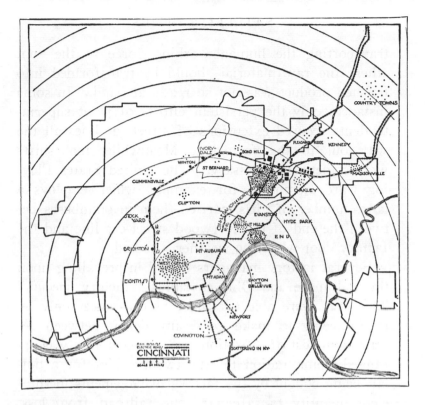

WHERE CINCINNATI SUBURBAN WORKERS LIVE

Each dot represents twenty workers. Data supplied by six factories covering 4,500 workers were taken as representative of the total number, about 10,000. Of these, nearly half or 44.68 per cent. were found to live in thickly populated parts of downtown Cincinnati, five miles from their work; about 5 per cent. lived still further away — across the river in Kentucky; only 31.28 per cent. were found to live in Norwood and Oakley.

transporting the human working force to the spot where the raw material should be transformed into finished product was not so ready at hand. In some instances only the persistent efforts of plant superintendents secured extensions of street-car lines all the way out to the factories. Meanwhile, makeshifts were sometimes necessary. The United States Playing Card Company, for example, which employs a large number of girls, carried them in omnibuses between the end of the Norwood street-car line and the factory door when the weather was bad.

Several factory managers united in prevailing upon the Baltimore and Ohio to run a " factory special." This they were able to secure at the outset only by guaranteeing to make good any deficit between receipts and cost of operation. A five-cent fare was arranged, commutation tickets, twenty rides for a dollar, being bought by the factory managements in sufficient quantity to safeguard the railroad from loss. These they resold to their employees.

To-day a ten-car train which starts almost empty when it leaves the Central Union Depot picks up its load at the stations at Eighth Street, Brighton and the Stock Yards, which tap the tenement districts of Cincinnati's West Side. Then, four miles out, at Cumminsville and St. Bernard, it gathers up others from regions of cheap, though not squalid, housing. With every seat taken, and aisles and platforms crowded, it travels on to the unloading stations, Norwood, East Norwood and Oakley. Oakley, nearly twelve miles from the Central Union Depot, is reached in about forty-five minutes. Leaving Oakley and Norwood at 5:45 each evening it drops its load at the various points along the line back to the Central Union Depot in Cincinnati where it arrives at 6:25 P. M. The service is not bad except for the insufficient number of seats during that portion of the trip in which the maximum load is carried.

The few Norwood and Oakley factory operatives who live in the country towns to the northwest are served by the Baltimore and Ohio, by two interurban lines and by the Cincinnati, Lebanon and Northern. The latter also carries some traffic out from its Cincinnati station on the edge of the central business district.

Street cars, however, afford the principal traction service between downtown Cincinnati and Norwood and Oakley. The trip, which takes twelve or fifteen minutes in the automobile of a factory official, requires from thirty-five to fifty minutes and longer for the factory worker who rides first on one line and then transfers. A five-cent fare covers the entire tributary area except Kentucky. The street-car company arranges to have several empty cars waiting near each factory at closing time. The rush for seats is partly due no doubt to the preference of many to take standing-room on the first few cars rather than wait for a seat in the cars behind. But even the latter are usually filled beyond their seating capacity. The ingenuity needed to make the whole inverted arrangement workable is illustrated by the fact that the playing card factory arranges for half of its seven hundred girl employees to start and quit work a quarter of an hour earlier than the other half. The afternoon distribution is also furthered by the fact that two hundred girls under eighteen years of age, and hence protected by the Ohio eight-hour law, leave work at 3 :45. Other plants allow the comparatively few women they employ to leave earlier than the men. But the latter, quitting all together, make a sudden and heavy demand on the street-car facilities.

The car lines to Norwood and Oakley appear to be a traction bonanza, with their full hauls both ways. The same cars which carry factory workers out at 7 :30 each morning are loaded on the way back with Cincinnati office workers going into the city. The reverse happens each afternoon.

But carfares figure on the other side of the ledger for the workers. Sixty cents a week is 10 per cent. of the $6 wage which is the average for many girls in Norwood factories.

The situation has thus created other social problems for managers and work-people than the simple one of human freightage. The willingness of employees to make the long trip twice a day was problematical. Yet so far from discouraging employees, the removal to the outskirts has been followed, most managers declare, by a longer average job tenure than was the case in Cincinnati. One manager said that although the well-lighted, ventilated, clean and roomy workshops

are an appreciated advantage, an important factor is
that workers have less opportunity to learn of new
jobs offering real or fancied betterment. Their contact with workers in other factories, with whom they
might compare work conditions and wages, is much
less frequent. At noon hours and on the way to and
from work they are now thrown only with those employed in the same factory, or else those employed in
near-by factories requiring a different kind of work.

In this connection it would be interesting to know
whether the evident success of employers in keeping
trade unionism weak in most of the Norwood and
Oakley factories is due in part to this isolation of the
workers from fellow-workers and trade-union representatives in the same industry. It is possible to discover not a little discontent among work-people in
various plants. The employment by one plant of some
negroes and " hunkies " is cited by other employees as
an effort to cut under the wage standards demanded
by " white men."

The longer journey to and from work seems to have
necessitated no reduction in work hours in order to hold
employees. Most of the plants run fifty five hours a
week, 7 A. M. to 5:30 P. M. each day except Saturday,
when noon is quitting time. The several hundred
girls at the United States Playing Card plant work, as
has been noted, a forty-eight- or forty-nine-hour week.
Those who tried to get the Ohio legislature to pass an
eight-hour law for women's work were disappointed
when the playing card company, which provides excel-

lent shop conditions, lined up with other manufacturers against any restrictions whatever. Incidentally, it is significant that in this plant 900 employees now turn out as large a product as 1,400 did a few years ago. This is, no doubt, due partly to new labor-saving machinery, but good work conditions are, doubtless, partly responsible. The plant management considers the main factor to be a premium and bonus system in connection with wage payments. This has meant somewhat higher wages, the premiums and bonuses being 10 per cent. of the total payroll expenditure.

Comparatively few operatives live near enough to go home for lunch. The facilities in the vicinity of the plants are poor. Some of the plants have established lunch-rooms. A plant which conducts an unusually good one, reports that it does so at a considerable annual loss. Some do not sell food but merely provide a place where lunches which are brought may be eaten, while others make provision only for the office force. But in most cases a work-bench, a curbstone, a doorstep or the nearest grassy spot must accommodate those who eat at the works, while several cheap and not very clean-looking saloons and "eating joints" serve crowds of others.

None of the industries found it necessary to increase wages on account of removal from downtown Cincinnati except the United States Playing Card Company. The comparatively small wages of its many girl employees were advanced 20 per cent. at the time of removal. Many of the employees paid carfare to reach their work when the factories were located in Cincinnati, so that for them the trip to Norwood, even if it means a longer street-car ride, does not add expense.

With these facts in mind why is it that Norwood and Oakley are not more largely peopled by the workers in their factories? Here are work opportunities, suburban surroundings usually coveted by city dwellers, and a long trip to and from work to be rid of. Why do so many of these workers continue to crowd into Cincinnati tenements?

The usual answer one gets is that many Norwood and Oakley workers are members of families whose principal breadwinners are employed in the factory center of Cincinnati and therefore want to continue to live near it. Or, it is said, that they like the bright lights and excitement of the big city. These do not seem adequate explanations. Other cities have downtown factory workers who live on the outskirts even without the inducement of suburban employment; and other small communities have provided sufficient zest in neighborhood and town life to interest the people who dwell there.

We may inquire, therefore, what efforts have been made to adapt this suburban area to the needs of the people brought together by its industries. If modern science and technical ability secured the highest degree of efficiency in plant arrangement and construction, have similar skill and ingenuity been applied to the community life, to town planning, housing, health and recreation?

As an example of foresight and efficiency in planning for manufacturing, the " factory colony " at Oakley is notable.　There was little concerted action in the industrial development at Norwood.　But Oakley has exhibited in remarkable degree the advantages which come through association.

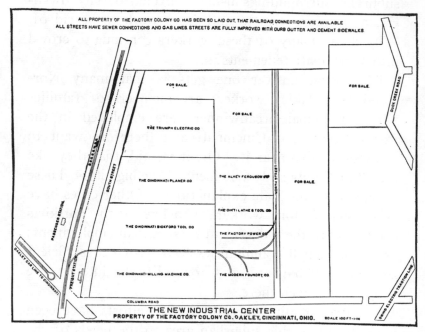

ALL PROPERTY OF THE FACTORY COLONY CO HAS BEEN SO LAID OUT, THAT RAILROAD CONNECTIONS ARE AVAILABLE
ALL STREETS HAVE SEWER CONNECTIONS AND GAS LINES. STREETS ARE FULLY IMPROVED WITH CURB GUTTER AND CEMENT SIDEWALKS.

FOR SALE.

FOR SALE.

FOR SALE

THE TRIUMPH ELECTRIC CO

THE CINCINNATI PLANER CO

THE ALVEY FERGUSON CO

FOR SALE

THE CINCINNATI LATHE & TOOL CO

THE CINCINNATI BICKFORD TOOL CO

THE FACTORY POWER CO

THE CINCINNATI MILLING MACHINE CO

THE MODERN FOUNDRY CO

THE NEW INDUSTRIAL CENTER
PROPERTY OF THE FACTORY COLONY CO. OAKLEY, CINCINNATI, OHIO.　SCALE 100 FT.-1-IN

THE " FACTORY COLONY "
Common power plant and foundry serve six factories

When the Cincinnati Milling Machine Company, in 1906, sought a new site away from Cincinnati's congestion, it found at Oakley some property used only for dairy and truck-gardening purposes.　The area was more than the company needed, and its charter did not permit it to deal in real estate. Accordingly, it interested several other factory managements in the organization of the Factory Colony Company. Space has been apportioned on the basis of " first come, first served," and six plants have been built. Five moved out from Cincinnati, and one came from Louisville.

The scheme has gone further and developed common means for supplying common needs through the organization of the Factory Power Company and the Modern Foundry Company, both owned by the group of factories and operated at cost. In the power company each factory has an interest proportionate to the service secured. This includes power, light, heat, water supply, compressed air, steam and pressure for sprinkler systems for fire protection. What this means in economy may be gauged from the fact that one of the plants now gets power at one and one-half cents per kilowatt hour. In its old location in Cincinnati it paid three cents. The power plant is laid out for a capacity of more than four times the present installation.

The Modern Foundry Company in a similar way serves the needs of the various plants. Through the specifications agreed upon for the construction of all the factory buildings, and through such other uniform conditions as the provision of a sprinkler system, insurance costs have been reduced to about one-tenth of what was paid on the old plants in Cincinnati.

Compared with this thought-out, well-joined, crafts-man-like organization of equipment to meet the common needs of these various manufactories, organization to meet the common needs of the people who run them, or the lack of it, in Norwood and Oakley presents a marked contrast. Only the scantiest attention has been given to it, even when the arrival of industries seemed to assure rapid town growth. Irregular farm boundaries had been allowed to determine streets and lines of growth. Large tracts owned by one man or his heirs, and held vacant for speculation, have hampered development. Subdivisions have been laid out without any reference to each other, and the whole arrangement of the town had the appearance of a crazy quilt, to quote the chairman of a platting commission which was established as early as 1889.

Through the commission's efforts a few streets were straightened, widened or vacated, and new ones platted with some reference to a general plan. But the lack of authority to cope adequately with the situation led this same man to declare that only " sweeping power " given to a county platting commission could protect the generations that are to follow from the selfishness of those bent on reaping profits from land regardless of the welfare of others — a remark well-nigh prophetic of the spirit which gave England a town planning act in 1909, and which must be stimulated in America if our cities are to have real opportunity to guide their suburban development.

This warning of nearly twenty years ago seems never to have been heeded. Subdivisions are still laid

out in Norwood and Oakley in any way that suits the
owner, provided the directions and widths of streets in
the older adjoining subdivisions are followed. Size
of lots, building lines, and other important features are
subject in no way to public control, but are at the mercy
of special interest or civic stupidity. A far-sighted
policy of community development is entirely lacking.

This is indicated, for example, by the lot widths.
In older subdivisions these are fifty feet; in later ones
thirty to forty-five feet; and in those most recently
platted, twenty-five feet. This is not necessarily an
evil. If a width of twenty-five feet is adopted with a
view to scientific house grouping [1] it may even be emi-
nently wise. But the crowded parts of many of our
large cities will show what miserable congestion may
develop on narrow lots when no adequate building restrictions are provided. In Norwood, narrow and
narrower lot platting has simply followed on the
growth in population because large profits could be
secured from cutting a given piece of property into
more lots.

Similarly, scientific planning of street-paving
widths on a basis of street function, which has meant a
difference of a shilling a week rent on each house in
some English garden suburbs, is as little understood
and applied in Norwood as it is in the average residential subdivision of our large cities.[2]

[1] See "Model Towns in America," by Grosvenor Atterbury.
Scribner's Magazine, July, 1912.

[2] See "Width and Arrangement of Streets," by Charles Mulford Robinson, published by *Engineering News.*

Most of the industrial plants which stretch along
the outer edge of Norwood and Oakley have allowed
space enough for years of expansion. Ordinary
business foresight took care of this. The land owned
by the factories, both that already occupied and that
held vacant for future needs, is now worth more than
$4,000 an acre, according to estimates based on the
Norwood appraisements of 1910 and the opinions of
real-estate men. One of the most favorably located
of these factory sites cost, says the president of the
concern owning it, $1,000 an acre in 1900. This
would indicate that land values in the neighborhood
of the factories advanced at least 400 per cent. in the
twelve years after the factories began to move out to
Norwood.

The abode of industry was thus assured when land
was cheap. Similar assurance for homes for the
workers away from congested Cincinnati was nobody's
concern. Blame cannot fairly be heaped upon plant
managers for this lack of civic and social foresight
in the industrial shift from city center to suburb. The
problems connected with the removal of the plants
themselves were doubtless complicated and engrossing
enough to monopolize their attention. There was not
the clear responsibility which rests on the single industrial establishment that builds a town for its sole occupancy. Such experiences as those of Pullman have
made industrial leaders hesitate to embark on social
and civic experimentation further than the effective
manning of their plants demands. The situation lays

bare the need for civic leaders of larger vision than those of twelve years ago — for a city statesmanship that shall give community affairs the same degree of thought and foresight and constructive genius which the ablest men devote to private enterprise.

To afford a basis on which we may gauge the living opportunities which Norwood and Oakley offer their factory workers we must first know the extent of income from which rent and living costs must be paid.

According to federal census figures for 1909, Norwood factories had 507 salaried employees, and 3,907 wage-earners. The salaried employees earned $632,000, or an average of $1,246.55 a year. The wage-earners received in a year $2,081,000, or an average of $532.53 each. This amounts to an average weekly wage of $10.24, which probably has risen in some degree since 1909. The large number of girl employees at low wages — the seven hundred at the United States Playing Card plant earn at the present time an average of $6 a week each — tends to make the general average lower than the average amount received by the heads of families. Let us turn, therefore, to two large plants employing almost wholly men. One is in Norwood and the other in Oakley, and each employs nearly 1,000 men. Both of these factories employ principally skilled operatives. It will be seen from the following tables that roughly a quarter of these workmen earn $10 or under per week and that three-quarters earn an average of $15 or less.

Plant No. 1. Men

Weekly Earnings of Shop Employees

21.88 per cent. earn under $10 a week
52.69 per cent. earn from $10 to $15 a week
24.86 per cent. earn from $15 to $20 a week
.57 per cent. earn over $20 a week

———

100.00

Plant No. 2. Men

Weekly Earnings of Shop Employees

39.54 per cent. earn under $10 a week
40.63 per cent. earn from $10 to $15 a week
16.86 per cent. earn from $15 to $20 a week
2.97 per cent. earn over $20 a week

———

100.00

The cheapest housing accommodations in Norwood are three-room flats, varying from $12 to $20 per month according to location and convenience. A real-estate agent of many years' experience in Norwood roughly classified the town's housing as follows:

Rents in Norwood

2,000 three-room flats at $12 to $20 per month
1,200 four-room flats at $15 to $25 per month
800 five-room flats at $20 to $40 per month
500 five-room houses at $20 to $25 per month
500 six-room houses at $25 to $32 per month
800 seven-room houses at $30 to $35 per month
600 eight-room houses at $35 to $50 per month

These figures were considered by one Norwood citizen to be much lower than the facts would suggest, particularly so far as three-, four- and five-room flats are concerned. But, taking them as they stand, they show that the cheapest three-room flats cost approximately one-quarter of the income of a twelve-dollar-a-week wage-earner, while if he desires more than three rooms for his family the expense rises far above that proportion. Many families, of course, have more than one wage-earner, thus swelling the family income, but that fact makes it no easier for the head of a family in which the children are all young or going to school.

Ownership of houses in the suburbs near their work is even more impossible for the Norwood and Oakley employees. From the standpoint of risk in home ownership, they present, to be sure, a safer proposition than do most industrial towns, for there is a diversity of industries, and employment is not solely dependent upon the ups and downs of one business. Work seems to be comparatively steady rather than subject to the extremes of dull and heavy seasons as in the steel industry. And furthermore, the bulk of Cincinnati industries are near enough so that in case of lack of employment in Norwood or Oakley, a worker living in the suburb has recourse to whatever opportunities for work the larger city affords. But the fact is that despite the factory growth, Norwood and Oakley have developed as residential suburbs for Cincinnati's business and salaried men to an extent that has put home ownership in them beyond the reach of the average workingman.

Under present building operations in Norwood the minimum cost of a small home is about $3,500, of which $700 or $800 represents cost of a lot with thirty-five feet frontage. In a typical case $2,250 is borrowed from a building loan association to be paid back with interest in installments of $21 per month. In addition, a cash payment of $500 goes at the outset to the builder of the house, who carries on credit the remaining $750. This is paid in monthly installments of from $15 to $20. Thus, $500 down and $36 a month is the cheapest rate at which, under present conditions, houses may be purchased. Almost none of these houses are bought by employees of Norwood factories. A Cincinnati builder recently put up twenty-seven houses in Norwood, but not one was for a Norwood factory employee.

The situation at Oakley is practically the same: $300 to $500 down, and $30 monthly on the principal with interest at 6 per cent., being necessary to secure a six-room house, costing with land about $3,600. In many cases these houses both in Norwood and Oakley are arranged for the occupancy of two families, the owner living in one flat and renting the other.

Nor does an extensive housing scheme now being carried out in Oakley enable workmen in Oakley factories to live in the suburb, as seems to be the current impression in Cincinnati. When the factories moved to Oakley in 1907, a tract of 110 acres — the old Oakley race-track property which had fallen into disuse owing to adverse racing legislation in Ohio — was secured by the Oakley Park Company. It built and sold about 150 houses in three years, but of these less than ten were purchased by employees of the Oakley plants.

The agent frankly stated that he made no effort to interest factory employees since their wages were too low to permit them to occupy houses of the type built. Most of the house purchasers are salaried Cincinnati men who occupy one-half the house and rent the other half. On the thus far undeveloped property of the Oakley Park Company, extending almost to the gates of the Oakley factories, there is room for about five hundred more houses. The amazing unintelligence and cumbersomeness of our civic negligence is apparent in the fact that if present building plans are continued, these will afford practically no accommodation for the men and women who go to work there. They must continue, many of them, to dwell far away in congested Cincinnati, while workers in Cincinnati dwell in Oakley.

In view of the failure to develop housing for workers in these industrial suburbs it is an interesting fact that among middle-western cities of a similar size Cincinnati has the largest proportion of tenement dwellers. At a recent municipal exhibit in Cincinnati it was shown that in Toledo 4 per cent. of all families were living in houses for three or more families; in Indianapolis, 6 per cent.; in Detroit, 7 per cent.; in Columbus, 8 per cent.; in Cleveland, 13 per cent.; in Louisville, 17 per cent.; in Buffalo, 24 per cent.; and in Cincinnati, 44 per cent.

The failure of housing developments in Norwood and Oakley to meet the needs of the factory workers has been recognized in the efforts of one Cincinnati man, J. G. Schmidlapp. He is following in the lines of the Washington (D. C.) Sanitary Improvement Company, which, in the last fifteen years, has invested nearly $1,000,000 and erected 289 houses accommodating 578 families, yielding 5 per cent. annual return on $500,000 capital stock and earning a considerable annual surplus.

Mr. Schmidlapp has built several groups of workingmen's houses in Norwood and Oakley. These provide sanitary dwellings at a rent considerably lower than that prevailing in either suburb. Unfortunately each house is exactly like every other house in the solid rows of brick, and one fears that a few years of deterioration will make them almost as dismal as the city tenement.

One group contains nine houses, each having two apartments of four rooms. These rent for $3.75 a week in the end houses and $3.25 a week in the others. Some of the inside houses have three-room apartments at $2.25 a week. Each apartment has a bathroom and at the rear an outside porch. Rents in another group of fourteen houses are slightly higher owing to the provision of cellars. The cost is approximately $3,000 per house including land. In the policy of administration 5 per cent. is allowed for return on the investment, and 4 per cent. for expenses and depreciation. Among 104 applicants for apartments in the first two groups of these houses in Norwood, seventy-five were already living in Norwood, seventeen were living elsewhere nearby, and twelve were living in Cincinnati. This would seem discouraging from the standpoint of inviting people away from congested areas, but the natural explanation given is that dwellers in Norwood had become familiar with the houses during construction and were eager to avail themselves of accommodations much less expensive than those they had been occupying.

The most distinctive feature of Mr. Schmidlapp's plan is his method of selling a two-family house to a wage-earner.   He hopes that the income from renting half the house will enable a workman to buy his home when he could not afford to buy a one-family house.

The building expense of a double house is of course less than twice the expense of a detached dwelling; the land area and taxes are also less; the workman who takes up the opportunity spends time and interest in keeping the property in good condition and keeping it rented; and he gets for his pains the profits in rentals and increased land values on the extra half of his property which would otherwise go to a real-estate company or large investor.   In other words Mr. Schmidlapp hopes to change workmen from renters to home-owners by getting them the benefits of one-ply landlords in the process.   The plan will, he doubtless feels, increase the number of citizens whose property gives them a conservative interest and permanent stake in the community.   He believes that he can turn over a

two-family house, after payments of about ten years,
on the following basis:

House having 2 three-room apartments, $100 cash and
$4.50 weekly

House having 2 four-room apartments, $200 cash and
$5.00 weekly

House having 2 five-room apartments, $300 cash and
$5.50 weekly

The original deposit is to be returned in case of
death or in case of disability compelling the purchaser
to give up his contract, when such disability is not the
fault of the purchaser.

These "philanthropy and 5 per cent." enterprises are
being watched with considerable interest by real-estate
men in Cincinnati and vicinity. Those in Norwood
and Oakley, however, have thus far shown no disposi-
tion to undertake similar enterprises, and the higher
profits to be made in building homes for Cincinnati
business and salaried men will likely monopolize their
attention in any event. Mr. Schmidlapp's influence
will count for most in demonstrating the possibilities
of safe long-term investment in the housing field by
the executors of estates and other trust funds.

Local builders have yet to be convinced that the
scheme is practicable; and some of them express their
opinion that it will make factory superintendents com-
placent in paying wages no higher than at present, and
perhaps even lower, in the belief that a workingman
will now have an opportunity to secure housing at low
rentals. These critics, admitting that their contention

is sound, perhaps lose sight of the fact that even if many more groups of houses are built by Mr. Schmidlapp, they can accommodate only a very small proportion of the total working force at Norwood and Oakley.

Social observers appreciate the value of his effort to provide thoroughly sanitary homes at a minimum of expense. One could wish, however, that even without reaching so low a rental figure, more pains had been taken to avoid a barracks-like monotony of structure. It is encouraging to know that his plans for the future promise more attractive dwellings, both Mr. Schmidlapp and his architect having devoted study to secure more variety in exterior appearance, greater convenience in floor plans, and better arrangement in the grouping of the houses.

The English garden suburbs, and some suburbs in this country as well, go to show that it is possible to provide much more attractive homes at very slightly higher cost. If wages reasonably within reach of the average workman are not sufficient to support a reasonable standard of comfort and charm in the home life of the people, the task of lowering the household standard to meet the wage scale may be a bottomless process; and constructive philanthropy could better apply itself to bringing up wage scales to a point where normal household life can be obtained under modern conditions. Given normal standards in house construction, the man who applies business acumen, the methods of large-scale construction and the gains of interest and increased land values to bring them within the reach of the average worker and lessen their strain on his household budget is doing a large public service.

There is general complaint that food costs as well as rent are high in these suburbs in comparison with Cincinnati and even with other suburbs. A study of the prices at four grocery stores — one in Norwood, one middle-class store in Cincinnati, one near the public market in Cincinnati, and one conducted by a firm which operates many stores in the poorer sections of the city — shows that, while there is no great discrepancy, Norwood prices were almost uniformly higher. Cincinnati is one of the few cities in this country which has extensively provided public markets. This fact doubtless led Norwood to build an excellent public market building. Stalls are rented at nominal fees, but for reasons not very obvious, the anticipated lessening of food costs has not resulted.

An effort to work out a coöperative living scheme for working girls was recently started by the Schmidlapp Bureau for Women and Girls. The bureau was founded by Mr. Schmidlapp as a memorial to his daughter, and he has given it an endowment of $500,000. Its work is educational, employment-finding and vocational. It provides financial aid for young women to complete their education; it finds work, and studies the industrial experiences of each girl and the problems of her social environment; and through pioneer research it is seeking to provide scientific data concerning vocational guidance. The director of the bureau is M. Edith Campbell, formerly in the Economics Department of the University of Cincinnati, and under her expert control the bureau is taking an important place among the movements toward social advance in Cincinnati.   She was recently elected a member of the Cincinnati School Board.

The Schmidlapp Bureau shares with the Union Savings Bank and Trust Company the management of the Schmidlapp houses already described.   It was in one of these house groups that two apartments were thrown into one, and a group of working girls gathered together in a coöperative household " club," supervised by a trained domestic-science teacher.   With the exception of a weekly house-cleaning the household work was shared by the girls.   Each member paid one dollar per week rent and two dollars for board.

Difficulty was experienced from the start in getting a group of unattached girls together in Norwood to try the experiment.   This was in part due, no doubt, to the policy of the United States Playing Card Company in employing girls living at home.

The stolid reason for this policy is that it helps safeguard the force from demoralizing influences, and there would obviously be no need for coöperative households if all girls were so placed.   But for the self-respecting girl living alone and solely dependent upon her own efforts the policy only serves to increase the difficulties of finding work, and there can be no doubt that it is an important money-saver for the company, so far as the payroll is concerned.   The willingness of girls living with their families to accept lower wages than they otherwise would operates most cruelly in fixing a lower wage standard for all working girls.

The furnishings of the home were given by Mr. Schmidlapp, whose interest in the experiment is three-fold: To provide a comfortable place for the self-supporting girl working in Norwood where there is now practically no inexpensive boarding place; to attempt to furnish under trained supervision simple but nourishing food for two dollars per person per week, and to teach the careful and economical management of a home.

Standards of living are not wholly matters of rent and meals.

A Norwood plant manager, who complained a little because it was so hard to get employees to come out to his establishment, was asked a few minutes later how he liked the advantages of the suburban location for his work.   " They are all right," he said, " but I find it hard to keep up the old interests and associations which mean a lot to me.   I don't have the same chance to run across old friends and join in the things at the club."

A social worker who knows what discouragement attends the efforts to persuade " city " girls to live in the working girls' " club," and " city " people to dwell in the Schmidlapp houses, expressed doubt whether " tons " of amusements would alter this.   " They simply will not leave the city *life* which you can never make in a suburb," she said.

Desire to live where " things are doing," near the bright lights, street crowds, big stores and amusements of the city center, and where friends are close at hand, is, after all is said, an important reason why many Norwood and Oakley workers do not make more of an effort to live where they work. The flats and apartment houses near the downtown section of almost any large city testify to the same sort of craving on the part of better-to-do people who find metropolitan advantages more to their liking than the quiet routine and distance from friends which the suburb enjoins. Theaters, opera, the life of the large hotels and the pleasures of the " smart set " have quite as strong a grip upon them as the cheaper amusements and " thrills " have upon the working people. Most of us have a yearning for sociability.

It is easy to say that working people cannot be tempted to live in the better conditions of the suburbs, that they find it too stupid and quiet. But this is just where our civic intelligence is challenged and where our planning falls short. If it is worth while as a civic policy to encourage escape from congestion to better and healthier living conditions, it is worth while to study out and provide means whereby recreation and neighborship can be stimulated centrifugally.

No such attention seems to have been given to recreation in Norwood and Oakley. There is a small playground, but it has poor leadership. A few band concerts are held each summer in front of the town hall, and baseball games are played between teams representing the different factories. A night school with from 350 to 400 attendants provides cooking, sewing and gymnasium work in addition to the common school subjects. The board of education also in response to a petition from some of the factory workers opened evening gymnasium classes in a school near the factories.

But in general the public recreation of the community is left to commercial enterprise. It consists of two motion-picture shows, one air dome, a baseball park for the games of a Saturday afternoon league, and a few bowling alleys and poolrooms mostly connected with saloons. Lack of any good-sized hall for entertainments, lectures, mass-meetings and social gatherings led, however, to an agitation to meet this need in a new city hall.

The school authorities are aware of the value of utilizing their school buildings for evening social and civic centers, but they point out that there are very few organizations to make use of them. Even the neighborhood " welfare societies " which took a great interest in the early civic problems of the community have nearly all died out or become inactive as municipal service has become more adequate. The possibilities of stimulating civic and social organization through social and recreation centers seem unknown. One neighborhood recreation center such as Chicago now has to the number of twenty-five might, with intelligent leadership, solve the problem. How small a proportion of the community's energy and money goes into public recreation is shown in a recent municipal report; a grand total of $140 is entered for public parks, covering only the playground above mentioned and inadequate for that, and $40,674 stands opposite police and fire departments.

While Norwood has not adapted its community life to serve the needs of an industrial population, so far as town planning, housing and recreation are concerned, some branches of public service are well provided. Her school system is considered unusually good. Her health is her proudest boast, though the 1912 budget of $2,040 for this purpose betokens no especial effort to conserve it and prevent dangers which would undoubtedly creep in with congestion. Water supply is of good quality, but said to be inadequate, particularly for industrial use. The rates are 7½ cents per hundred cubic feet, with 75 cents as a minimum quarterly charge. The water works are municipally owned as is also the electric-light plant which supplies light at 6 cents per thousand watts as compared with the Cincinnati rate of 8 cents. Street car and telephone franchises have provoked no serious struggles, but Norwood has had to accept practically the same terms as Cincinnati. In 1900 when a new street-car franchise was negotiated, the duration was made uniform with Cincinnati franchises, but two extensions of lines and a five-cent fare to any point in Cincinnati by universal transfers were secured.

In the handling of the gas situation this town has really shown its power. Norwood secured striking

advantage not only for her own citizens, but for all
Cincinnati. The rate in Cincinnati had been 75 cents
a thousand feet, and this was the rate which the Cincinnati company also charged the suburb. The Norwood city council encouraged an Ohio company to
pipe in natural gas at 25 cents per thousand feet. To
meet the competition the Cincinnati company found itself compelled to pipe in natural gas from West Vir-
ginia. The Ohio company then sold out its rights to
the Cincinnati company, but not before the citizens saw
to it that the price should remain as low as 30 cents.
Cincinnati was thus, through Norwood's civic alert-
ness, enabled to secure its supply at less than half the
rate it formerly paid.

Annexation to Cincinnati has thus far been successfully opposed by Norwood which recently voted against
it by 2,759 to 930, while Cincinnati voted 5 to 1 for
it. But Oakley voted for annexation.

Norwood's chief argument in opposition is the fear
of putting good neighborhood conditions at the mercy
of a gang-ridden city. This was for a time counter-
acted by Cincinnati's election of Henry T. Hunt as
mayor, an able young reformer who gave the city an
efficient administration. " When Cincinnati gives evidence that her reform is permanent, and when she goes
in for such things as parks and schools for her whole
population, we'll be glad to come in," said a fair-
minded Norwood citizen who has consistently opposed
annexation. Norwood's contention that under annexation there would be no assurance as to how much

of her taxes would be spent locally is answered by the fact that the expense of serving territory annexed in 1911 would be $272,329, or more than three times the revenue, $86,284, to be obtained from such territory.

The broad handling of the town planning, housing and transportation conditions in these industrial suburbs, involving the relation of industries to residential areas, demands first of all a program of construction and public control in the interests of the whole body of people who live and work in them. Each community needs civic coherence. What can be done by concerted action has been shown in the " factory colony," in the Schmidlapp housing enterprise, and in the fight for gas. The need, however, is wider than this. The complexities of modern life which have made citizens so interdependent upon each other for their mutual welfare have also made the towns and flanges of a metropolitan district interdependent. Each locality has much to gain from a comprehensive plan including all, and each has something to contribute, just as Norwood's efforts gave to the whole people of Cincinnati the boon of cheap lighting.

The exodus of industry from the congested center of Cincinnati has shown us no comprehensive and intelligent civic policy on the part of the big city to promote and guide community development. Equally in their smaller spheres, Norwood and Oakley have failed.

If the same degree of forethought, skill, intelligence and enterprise, which was applied to the planning of the " factory colony," had also been applied to the

scheming of the community life of Oakley and Norwood, the environs of Cincinnati might now have developed the most interesting and significant industrial
suburbs in America, might even have shown us our
nearest approach to the garden suburbs of England in
point of coöperative land ownership and building as
well as in physical arrangement. With broad fields,
trees, gentle hillsides, and a ravine with a water course,
nature has done her part to provide beauty. But, except in the efforts of Mr. Schmidlapp, not the slightest attempt has been made to solve the problem of the
workers' household in these surroundings near his
work. The recreation of the working girl seems to
have received scarcely a thought. The removal of
the factory to the rim of the big city is not an adequate
solution of our civic-industrial problem if it leaves the
workers' home behind in a congested area, or even if
it transplants it to a region where the whole system of
community life is left to remain undeveloped.

The intelligence which is so skillfully applied to the
planning of industrial expansion should be directed to
the great opportunity for guiding civic and social development in the outer belts of growth.

CHAPTER V

ECONOMIC GAIN AND CIVIC ISOLATION

The "East Side" has come to be almost synonymous with social and civic problems. St. Louis applies the term to the string of towns sprawled along the opposite bank of the great river, and it is appropriate in its civic as well as its geographical connection. But while New York's East Side has problems of incrusted congestion, St. Louis' East Side consists of comparatively new satellites, their growth so much in process that its shaping is both possible and worth while.

Industrial suburbs commonly have had to strike new civic root at a distance from the established community life of the large center. But these St. Louis satellites present this problem in accentuated form. Special dividing lines across which industry jumped to secure unusual economic gains have meant unusual civic isolation. The Mississippi has been a great barrier to the flow of life between the East Side suburbs and the big city. And the intervening state line separates fields for citizenship into divided fields of action, with little opportunity for associated civic effort.

These Illinois towns are linked to the larger city by four big coupling pins — the bridges across the broad, brown Mississippi. Directly facing St. Louis, and as close to the river bank as a network of railway terminals will permit, is an agglomeration of business buildings, dwellings, and tall chimneyed industrial plants. This is East St. Louis, linked to the city proper by two bridges. On its northern edge between a sluggish, dirty stream and some railroad tracks are extensive stockyards. Beyond stretches a swampy area, crisscrossed with railways and dotted with occasional factories and houses. Still farther north, where the third bridge leads over from St. Louis, the settled area peters out into straggling houses and hovels. This is Venice, unkempt, amphibious.

The trolley cars from across the bridge spend little time on their way through Venice to another and larger community set to the northeast a mile or two back from the river bank. Like a huge city wall, the big manufacturing plants are ranged along its western edge, while the stacks of a steel mill serve as sentinels to the east. The first section that the cars enter is made up of miscellaneous small houses with occasional ugly larger buildings. This is Madison. You go on into a better set-up section, Granite City, which is slowly creeping out into the prairie with skirmish lines of box-like dwellings. To one side is a forlorn neighborhood beyond the western bulwark of industries and railroads. This is " Hungary Hollow."

East St. Louis, Madison, and Granite City are not an overflow of St. Louis industry — for few factories have actually shifted their location from one side of the river to the other. But the modern tendency to utilize industrially the outskirts of large centers of population has here been based not alone on the factors which commonly operate. The special economic advantages, some of them arbitrary and artificial, are shared by all three Illinois towns over St. Louis. St. Louis has been reluctant to admit that such advantages existed. Until recently her principal commercial body would rather have thrown a new industry to Kansas City, nearly three hundred miles away, but in the same state, than to any one of the Illinois towns just across the river.

But the last few years have seen the beginnings of a new spirit; the old jealousies are being laid aside, and the real unity of the metropolitan industrial district is becoming recognized on both sides of the river. In seeking to bring in new industries, the Business Men's League of St. Louis, which is increasingly representative of the Illinois as well as the Missouri side, now seeks to explain fairly the relative advantages of locating in St. Louis proper, on its western outskirts, or in the towns of the East Side. Many plants find that St. Louis sites, with better sewerage and the cheap power from the dam across the Mississippi at Keokuk, are preferable to those with the advantages of the East Side.

Some of the advantages of the East Side over St. Louis are those which the periphery of any large center of population usually possesses:

1. Cheap Land. Large level tracts are available in East St. Louis within twenty-five minutes from the

St. Louis business district. Although the fare is ten
cents it is expected to be reduced to five cents soon.
The nearest similar tracts on the western outskirts of
St. Louis are at least an hour away by street-car.
East Side sites cost usually less than half as much as
those in St. Louis.

2. Railroad Facilities. East St. Louis is a notable
railway center.

3. Proximity to Labor Supply. St. Louis workingmen's districts are within street-car distance of East
Side plants.

But the East Side's peculiar advantages over St.
Louis are of a sort not usually possessed by the outskirts of big cities.

1. Cheap Fuel. This, as important as cheap land, is
due to an " arbitrary " whereby the Terminal Railroad
Association charges on a ton of coal from the great
Illinois bituminous mines from 10 to 100 miles away
a uniform rate of fifty-two cents to St. Louis, and only
thirty-two cents to any point on the East Side.

2. Cheap Water. Large quantities for manufacturing purposes cost less than half as much as in St. Louis.

3. Differences in Laws. The absence of smoke regulation such as that in St. Louis is said to be an advantage for the heavy coal-consuming industries of the
East Side. But East Side manufacturers point to the
fact that they are seeking fuel economy through the
elimination of smoke. Labor conditions do not seem
to be affected much by the differences in labor legislation. Missouri has a nine-hour day and fifty-four-

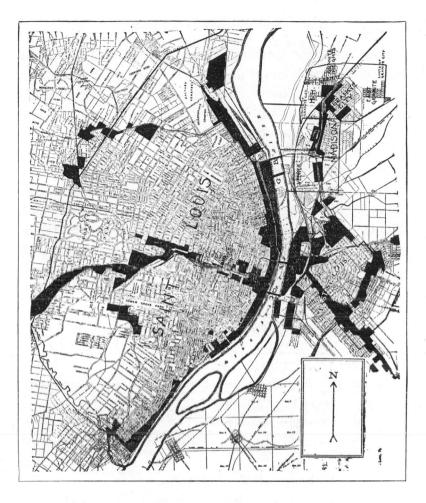

ST. LOUIS INDUSTRIAL DISTRICT

Black indicates principal areas devoted to industrial purposes.
Bridges: A — Eads Bridge. B — Merchants'. C — McKinley.
D — Incompleted Free Bridge.

hour week for working women, while the Illinois law provides ten hours a day and sixty hours a week as a maximum. Illinois has a workman's compensation law, while Missouri hoped to get one at the 1915 session of the legislature, but failed.

The "arbitrary" on coal is part and parcel of the one great civic issue which for years has stirred St. Louis into bitter struggle. The Terminal Railroad Association, including most of the railroads which enter the city, controls all the railway and ferry facilities crossing the river, and the belt lines serving both sides. It contends that costly bridges warrant the high freight toll across the river, and that a flat rate of twenty cents a ton is better for the city as a whole than a mileage rate to points of delivery in St. Louis. Many St. Louis citizens, however, feel that aside from whether the terminal association itself or the railways composing it make excessive profits, public necessity demands relief for the whole city. The shippers were the first to organize a remedial effort. Under the leadership of David R. Francis they built the Merchants' Bridge in 1889. But in a few years this passed to the control of the terminal association.

The second development came a few years ago. The McKinley traction lines, with 580 miles of ramifications in Illinois, built a bridge. But it connects with no belt-line facilities for distribution in St. Louis, and so has had little effect. The McKinley interests filed a forty-two-cent rate and asked the St. Louis Municipal Assembly to give it a franchise to connect with the

belt lines of the terminal association.   But public
sentiment was suspicious, and the assembly refused to
give the franchise unless an agreement should be
made to abolish the " arbitrary " entirely and
bring the rate down to thirty-two cents or a mileage
basis.

St. Louis' hope has been staked on the third enterprise, the Free Bridge, built by the municipality with
$3,500,000 obtained through the issuance of bonds in
1906.   An additional bond issue of $2,750,000 to com-
plete the approaches to the bridge was authorized by
the voters in November, 1914, after three previous defeats which had tied up the project for over three
years.   The defeats were due largely to the fear that
the East Side approaches were not sufficiently beyond
the reach of terminal association control.   Meanwhile,
a perfectly good bridge was about as useless a public
convenience as could be imagined since only one end
was connected with the land.   For years, therefore, despite St. Louis' efforts to secure the same rate, the East
Side has enjoyed a purely artificial advantage in the
cost of coal.

Cheap land and cheap coal have thus been the greatest factors in attracting industries for which one or
both are important.   In the removal of the St. Louis
stockyards to East St. Louis, for instance, cheap land
was of course the main consideration.   So it was in
the development of the railway yards and terminals
on the Illinois side.   But in the heavy steel manufacturing which plays so important a part in the develop-

ment of the whole East Side, cheap land in large tracts
and a large supply of cheap coal are prime factors.
The East Side has rapidly become, therefore, the section of the St. Louis industrial district into which
heavy industrial processes, usually the dirtiest and
dingiest, have been shunted.

A FACTOR IN CIVIC ISOLATION

Although built to relieve St. Louis from high freight rates,
citizens refused for years to vote for the completion of the Free
Bridge, fearing railroad control of the Illinois approach.

In 1890 East St. Louis had but 15,169 population
while Granite City and Madison did not show at all
in the census returns.   The growth from 1900 to 1910
shows the later developments of the East Side:

	1900	1910
East St. Louis	29,655	58,547
Granite City	3,122	9,903
Madison	1,979	5,046
Venice	2,450	3,718

In 1912 East St. Louis was estimated to have about 70,000 people, and Granite City — the 1910 census of which omitted two wards — about 12,000. The growth of this group of towns from 1900 to 1910 was no less than 108 per cent. St. Louis in the same decade increased only from 575,238 to 687,029, a growth of but 19 per cent. For a comparison of East Side growth with that of the western outskirts of St. Louis the data are not available.

Venice shows little growth. Its low situation exposes it particularly to the annual high water in the Mississippi. This makes it undesirable for manufacturing sites, but railroad yards are expected to occupy parts of its territory. Formerly a little settlement at a ferry station, it is now a forlorn collection of ramshackle houses clustered around the approach to the McKinley Bridge, though its appearance has recently shown some improvement, particularly since it now boasts a well-paved main street. Along the river-bottoms its amphibious dwellings — shanties on scows, at home floating on the flood or grounded wherever the subsiding waters leave them — give a picturesque touch to its squalor. While its recurring inundations led it to claim its name, one could scarcely imagine a more incongruous contrast with the Queen of the Adriatic.

The flood danger which has been so great a handicap to the whole East Side is now less menacing through the recent construction of a great levee at a cost of $6,500,000 in which all the East Side communities shared.

To the social observer interested in the civic and community aspects of suburban industrial developments, these East Side towns present an interesting and somewhat different situation from that which is usually to be found on the outskirts of a big city. They are separated from the central metropolis of their industrial district by a great river and by a state line; they have, as has been pointed out, more than the ordinary economic advantages over it; they share its general destiny but comparatively little of its civic life.

The situation can be seen more distinctly by focusing attention on a typical community. Granite City is not only a community by itself and typical in that all the economic factors mentioned above affect it, but it has added significance in the fact that its establishment and development were definitely planned at the outset by one large industrial interest. The share taken by immigrants in its life may also be measured the more easily since " Hungary Hollow," where they are massed, is an isolated part of the town. Furthermore, distinctive labor conditions, involving union organization and reduced hours of work, add special interest to it as a community.

The newcomer wonders half-consciously how the name Granite City became attached to a place located

on the soft soil of a great river valley.   The manufacture of enameled " granite " kitchenware christened
the place.   It was in 1893 that F. G. and W. F. Niedringhaus selected the spot and bought 4,000 acres to
provide a town for their granite-ware factory, which

AT HOME ON LAND OR WATER
Venice, Illinois, frequently flooded by the Mississippi, has many
amphibious dwellings. The major part of the town now
has levee protection.

had outgrown its site in St. Louis.   This is the only
plant in Granite City which may be said to have moved
over from St. Louis.   The other industries which now
help to employ 8,500 workers in Granite City started
there, largely through the initiative of the Niedringhauses.   They were especially interested in starting

the large plants of the American Steel Foundries and the Commonwealth Steel Company

At the outset the company platted the town, improved the streets, provided sewers and water supply, planted 14,000 trees, and built one hundred houses, including fifty double ones of brick. In 1896 the place was incorporated as a city. In 1912, with over 12,000 inhabitants, it boasted the following principal plants:

National Enameling & Stamping Co. (steel works),
   employing 1,800
National Enameling & Stamping Co. (stamping
   works), employing 1,000
American Steel Foundries, employing............ 1,700
Commonwealth Steel Co., employing............. 2,900
National Lead Co., employing.................. 600
Corn Products Refining Co. and other industries,
   employing 500

The yearly payroll is estimated at $6,500,000. Of the 8,500 workers, it is estimated that 65 per cent. live in Granite City and 35 per cent. in St. Louis.

The selection of the town site on land as high as could be found in the river lowlands was the most important factor in its planning. This was clearly shown in 1903, when floods covered the whole area for miles around, but left Granite City and the major part of East St. Louis untouched. The streets were laid out in the customary gridiron arrangement, except that one diagonal thoroughfare was provided from the stamping and enameling plant through the business center to

a residential district in the opposite corner.   This avenue bears the name of the town's founder.   His sons
wanted the town itself to be known as " Niedringhaus,"
but he objected.   It may be that the notoriety in which
the town of Pullman found itself that very summer
had something to do with his stand, for he watched
keenly the developments in Chicago's paternalistic
satellite.   Indeed, the Pullman strike and the bearing
which company house rentals had upon it are said to
have materially modified the elder Niedringhaus'
scheme for Granite City.

Lots were given a width of fifty feet·in the original
plat.   In some of the more recent subdivisions real-
estate companies have cut the width in two for the
purpose, they say, of bringing the cost of homes within
the means of less skilled workmen.   While the real-
estate company formed by the Niedringhauses has continued to be active, considerable tracts of land were
sold to other companies for development.   The companies claim that lots are sold at only a reasonable
profit, but there is a somewhat prevalent impression
among the people that all the companies have made a
" good thing " out of the land values which the influx
of population has created.   " Why, they could operate
the plants at a loss and still make money because of the
land," is the way one man expressed his opinion.   But
the Niedringhaus company pursues a policy of disposing of its real estate as rapidly as possible, and declares that its realty company has never paid a dividend.

From the figures given by one of the principal real-estate dealers it would appear that land profits have not been small. The original value before the town was built was about $500 an acre, though for parts it was as low as $150 an acre. An acre makes about five lots fifty feet wide. Lots in the best residence sections sell to-day at an average of $1,000, many of them being worth as much as $1,500, while most of those in the poorer sections are valued at $300 and up. Some of the twenty-five-feet lots and a few of the poorest larger ones sell for as low as $150. It will be seen that the advance in values in the nineteen years since the town was established has been great. And indeed this same real-estate dealer estimated that the last four years alone have seen an advance of 100 per cent. But a home-owner expressed the opinion that average lot prices in the central part of the town are even higher than the figures cited.

A factor in boosting land values has, of course, been the construction of the levee, for land hitherto worthless because submerged nearly every spring has now been redeemed from this disadvantage. The lowest land just back of the levee, for example, once worth $40 an acre is now worth $1,000, according to the real-estate dealer already quoted. The assessments for the levee were spread over a large area so that on the average the apportionment amounted to only about $2.40 per $1,000 on the previously assessed valuation.

The original purchase of land for the town included large holdings near the river so that the increase in valuation of the protected portion may be surmised. Two thousand acres along the river bank and not protected by the levee are held by the Niedringhaus interests.   They were originally secured to protect Granite City from the development of inferior towns between it and the river.   Their future value is dependent on East Side development sufficient to warrant river-bank improvement and an additional levee.

A third factor in determining land values is the McKinley Bridge, across which the interurban lines have now been running for several years.   Prior to this time, except for the special morning and evening trains which, at the urgency of the manufacturers, the terminal association ran with a five-cent fare, the journey from the heart of St. Louis was by way of East St. Louis and involved twenty cents carfare to say nothing of an hour's experience resembling that to be had for a nickel on a " scenic railway."   By way of the McKinley Bridge a five-cent fare takes one from Granite City to the heart of the St. Louis business district in about thirty-five minutes, and cars run ten minutes apart.

One would think that the former inadequate transportation would have caused St. Louis workmen employed at Granite City to move there and that the present ease and cheapness of living in St. Louis and working in Granite City would tend to discourage removal to Granite City.   But the actual movement of population appears to be the other way.   A real-estate dealer sold 350 lots in six weeks in a new subdivision shortly after the McKinley Bridge went into operation and 75 per cent. of them were to St. Louis residents who had been working in Granite City. He adduces the further evidence that there is not a vacant store or house in the town now though there were always some before.

The increased security in land ownership due to the fact that Granite City dwellers can now easily reach employment in St. Louis if the home industries have slack periods is no doubt one of the factors in the increased sale of Granite City land. This same fact, of course, makes it easy for sons and daughters of a man employed in a Granite City plant to take up office or store employment in St. Louis. It also means that St. Louis' resources for recreation, education and social life, as well as her stores, are within reach. Since the opening of the McKinley Bridge it has been estimated that 70 per cent. of the money earned in Granite City is spent in St. Louis. Yet the local stores are said to be in even a more prosperous condition than formerly because of the increase in the number of households, as workingmen move their families over from St. Louis.

In the last ten years nearly all the company houses have been sold to working people. They are double dwellings, not unattractive, and are built upon alternate lots, the original idea being that the occupants of each house might have a garden. As the lots in between become occupied by houses of varying appearance the monotony of a row of like houses will be broken. The sales were made on a basis of the original cost plus 6 per cent. a year.

Unlike the contract of sale of the Gary Land Company, there is no provision for buying houses back in case the occupant leaves Granite City. But the company has never foreclosed a mortgage. In three instances houses have been taken back and the purchase price returned. The sales of lots and houses by the real-estate companies have been in the ordinary way on time payments. Prior to 1913 more than 2,500 houses were built, and through twelve building and loan associations over $400,000 was loaned, most of the money coming from small country towns in the vicinity.

From the days in which the town's founders took pride in their encouragement of churches and schools Granite City has boasted of its provisions for these institutions. At the beginning a building site was given to each church. In church buildings more than $150,-000 has been invested, and citizens are accustomed to point out how much better morally Granite City is than Madison, its adjoining neighbor. Persistent efforts drove gambling from Granite City, and recently from Madison, and this evil is said now to come no nearer than Venice.

Six public schools afford the educational facilities for two thousand school children and the superintendent has guided the growth of the system since the time when he himself was the only teacher and had thirty-two pupils on the first day of school. In such ways as the provision of medical inspection the schools seem to be up to date. There is little social center work, however, though public lecture courses and night classes in the common branches are conducted.

A hospital erected and first managed by the Lutheran Hospital Association with the financial help of the Niedringhauses is now conducted under Catholic auspices and seems to be rendering efficient service. A group of ladies from the different churches is organized to meet some of the charitable and civic needs of the place.

Restriction of saloons was prominent in the minds of the elder Niedringhauses when the town was established, and their regulations still hold that the consent of the owners representing two-thirds of the lot-owners on a block must be secured before a saloon may be established in the block. This operated to keep the number of saloons down to about thirty-two. There was practically no increase for a period of five years prior to 1913. But the number then increased rapidly so that by the summer of 1914 there were fifty-two.

One small park was provided in the town's original plan, a little circle of formal flower beds at the intersection of streets in the center of the town. But neglect and abuse of this "beauty spot" caused it to be given up. No effort has been made even to plan ahead for a park system, as East St. Louis has done by calling in George E. Kessler as an expert. Outside of a few vacant places utilized as baseball fields, the recreation of Granite City is left to several nickel and ten-cent theaters and a public dance hall or two.   One club building is fairly well equipped to serve its members in a recreational way.   Only one industrial plant, that of the Commonwealth Steel Company, has a club house for its employees.   This has pool tables, a little gymnastic apparatus, a hall, shower baths and library.   A large lunch-room for the workmen is operated without profit, as well as a dining-room for superintendents and officials.   The same company also conducts a technical night school for its employees.

There is one most striking contrast in Granite City's community life.   Here is a town with the most meager provision for recreation, with only the beginnings of a public library and no Y. M. C. A.— a town singularly barren of means for the utilization of leisure.   Yet in this very place are to be found advanced labor experiments aimed at giving greater leisure to workingmen.   For some of the steel plants in Granite City have demonstrated, to the satisfaction of their officials, the economic advantages of three eight hour shifts as contrasted with two twelve-hour shifts in continuous processes.[1]   The Commonwealth Steel Company put its furnace and boiler crews on the three-shift plan.   According to the paper of General Superintendent R. A. Bull, read at a recent convention of the American Foundrymen's Association, the plant has actually saved money, for the waste and inefficiency due to negligence and fatigue are reduced enough to outweigh the 20 per cent. addition to the payroll of the men affected.

[1] *See* article in *The Survey,* November 16, 1912, p. 198.

The same testimony is enthusiastically given by Vice-President George W. Niedringhaus of the Granite City Steel Company, where there are a larger number of men working eight-hour turns than in any other Granite City Plant. The eight-hour shift was first applied in this plant to operations which are not necessarily continuous for metallurgical reasons. But it has recently been extended to the entire open-hearth department, and also to the Universal Mill where the bars are rolled.

When the eight-hour basis was first contemplated at the Commonwealth Steel Company's plant, difficulties were foreseen, some of them concerning the attitude of the employees toward necessary wage reductions. The change was accompanied by an average advance of 22 per cent. in hourly rate of wages, but the four-hour reduction meant that the daily wage decreased about 20 per cent. In view of this fact, the officials were very doubtful as to whether the eight-hour shift would meet with the approval of the men, but when the question was submitted to them, a unanimous affirmative vote was the result. The plan has thus worked out in a way satisfactory both to the men and to the managers of the plants, who feel that it is demonstrated to be economically sound.

Success, therefore, at the open-hearth platforms of these two companies are bound to have a considerable measure of influence not only in Granite City but throughout the country where the eight-hour shift is wholly at variance with general furnace practice.

" We want the time to be with our families and do odd jobs around the house," some of the open-hearth men said to Mr. Bull. And none of them has sought to use the free time in money-making side jobs, as some of the officials of steel-producing plants have contended would be the case with such a change. That there has been little bad use of the leisure the officials of the Granite City companies all agree. " Steel work is so strenuous," says Mr. Niedringhaus, " that any man who took to dissipation would be unable to keep up his efficiency even through the eight-hour shift. The fact that we do not have to discharge any of them shows in itself that the time is not badly spent." The success of the eight-hour shift in a city so poorly equipped for the use of leisure would seem to promise much if the schedule were inaugurated in communities where more adequate recreation facilities have been developed.

In this connection it is peculiarly interesting that the Granite City Steel Works presents one of the most strongly unionized steel-producing plants in the country. And officials almost without exception agree that this was an important factor in leading to the introduction of the shorter working shift. Ever since the days of the elder Niedringhauses, who firmly believed that through the unions they were apt to get the best men, yearly trade agreements have been effected between the Granite City Steel Works and the unions, including the Amalgamated Association of Sheet and Tin Plate Workers — the organization with which the

United States Steel Corporation has had one of its bitterest fights.

Organization recently extended to the girls employed at the enameling and stamping company plant and about one hundred out of the two hundred and fifty joined the union. This came about, according to some of those interested in the girls' organization, at the instance of the " burners " who had already secured the eight-hour day. To strengthen their own position the " burners " brought about the organization of the girls. The company has made no objection, although the Women's Trade Union League declares that a few years ago when it sought to organize the girls three of the leaders were discharged and a forelady warned the girls not to attend the meeting. Union organization is strongest in the Niedringhaus plants; the Commonwealth and American Steel Foundries' plants are only partly unionized, while the Corn Products Refining Company plant has practically no unionized employees. Of all Granite City workers perhaps one-third are organized.

The relations of the Granite City Steel Works with its unionized employees have recently developed into unusual and mutually advantageous coöperation. The company, anticipating a hard struggle because of business conditions and the new tariff law, laid the problem before the leaders of the men — stating that it did not wish to discharge men or cut down wages and that the men could help avoid such contingencies if they would assist by economizing material, power and time.

The response, according to Mr. Niedringhaus, was cordial and effective, and was especially gratifying in labor-union settlements during the summer of 1914.

With a member of the Amalgamated Association, a former worker in one of the local steel plants, serving for a time as mayor, elected on the Socialist ticket, labor questions appeared to be a factor in politics. Yet it was significant to find relations of personal cordiality between a mayor of this type and the head of the steel mill. The mayor, while of course critical of employers as a class, was glad to give the latter credit for being a fair and liberal employer. And similarly, the steel executive gave friendly recognition to the good personal qualities of the mayor, although doubting his ability to see all sides of community problems.

Aside from the strength which the Socialist party displayed during this period, the mayor has undoubtedly had some support from those who think that the industrial control has dominated too much the civic affairs of the town. They point to the land, to the gas company and one of the principal banks, in all of which the Niedringhaus interests are supreme. And they show how political control has also been in company hands through the election of its men as mayor and aldermen. Indeed, the Socialist mayor found himself confronted by a board of ten aldermen made up of three Niedringhaus employees, a painting contractor, a landlord, a saloon-keeper, a railway foreman, one

workingman from a foundry and only two Socialists.

That some company officials seek to dominate the
politics of the place seems clear.   One of the superintendents has for years been a factor in the local affairs of one national party and " deeply interested," to
quote his own words, in one of the municipal parties;
for it is a noteworthy fact that national party names
have played no part in local politics.   " I want to say
right now," he declared, " that people desire no more
Socialist mayors in Granite City."   To beat the mayor
for reëlection, this plant superintendent helped to
smooth out the factional differences and unite the two
older municipal parties in opposition to the Socialists.
A combination of all the anti-Socialists was finally well
organized and a campaign was conducted so successfully that in the election which followed the Socialists
were beaten three to one.

The mayor asserted that some of the business men
were afraid to voice their objections to the control of
the city by the Niedringhauses.   On the other hand,
nearly every business man will tell you what an " unfortunate thing it was for Granite City to be known to
outside capital as a Socialist city," although one heard
no word against the mayor as a man.   But the mayor
pointed out further that some of the most discerning of
his supporters were members of the Amalgamated who
had worked in other places and had observed what
steel companies are able to do if they control the machinery of local government.   It should be stated, how-

ever, that at no time has there been any serious antagonism between company and town over issues of civic importance.

Perhaps the most important social problem in Granite City is that presented by the picturesque and isolated mass of immigrants in " Hungary Hollow." No group in the community is more neglected, unless it be the negroes, of whom about 1,000 are employed in the plants. All the latter live, however, in near-by squalid towns since there is an unwritten law in Granite City that no one shall sell or rent real estate to negroes. Counting Granite City and Madison as one community it includes one of the largest settlements of Bulgarians and Macedonians to be found in this country.

There is no civic requirement in which American industrial communities fail more conspicuously than in their handling of the lowest paid immigrant labor. The very unwillingness of such towns to have their immigrant conditions described or considered as typical is evidence of this. Yet the fact that such labor is more essential in these towns than elsewhere warrants especial attention to the conditions under which immigrants live and work. " It is true," said a factory official, " that the district is an eyesore to Granite City, yet ' Hungary Hollow ' is necessary to the success of the large plants and the conditions are no different from those surrounding foreign communities in other cities. The large plants require common labor and Americans will not accept these positions." And then, as if to defend his city's prestige, he said, " Granite City is practically isolated from its foreigners and Americans do not mingle with them either socially or in a business way." But he pointed out some of the difficulties which surround efforts at betterment, by adding, " The majority are here to-day and gone to-morrow, adopt the least expensive mode of living and do not come to the United States with the intention of becoming American citizens."

To a description of the work and life of the Granite City Bulgarians and Macedonians the Federal Immigration Commission devoted much space in its report, and this document has been drawn upon for much of the information here set forth. It is estimated that in 1907 the number of Bulgarians reached 8,000, though some of the best informed citizens think this figure too large. But the general industrial depression of that year sent many back to the fatherland and reduced the number to only a few hundred. The group has since increased, although temporarily diminishing in the summers owing to the exodus for railway construction work. In the fall of 1912 as many as 600 went back to fight in the Balkan War. Of the 1,000 who were left, a large proportion lived in " Hungary Hollow." A further cause for their diminishing numbers is that plant superintendents have declared the Macedonians unsatisfactory workmen. One man said he would rather have two negroes than three Macedonians.

More than 90 per cent. are men — some single, but many with families in the old country. More than 90 per cent. have been in this country less than five years.

About 61 per cent. are employed in the steel plants, but less than 3 per cent. are affiliated with trade unions. While their sobriety is said to be above the average American standard, they are not adaptable in their work, require much supervision and are generally the least effective industrially of the immigrant races.

A MACEDONIAN SALOON IN "HUNGARY HOLLOW"

But increasingly the younger men who have some intention of staying in this country attend school.

Their earnings are from fifteen to nineteen cents per hour for common labor, and some of them on piece work in other departments earn as much as thirty cents or more. At the time of the Immigration Commission study, practically all earned less than $600 a year; nearly 92 per cent. less than $400; and about 25 per cent. less than $200; these figures would now probably be from 10 to 15 per cent. higher with the present

higher rate of wages. But in addition account must
be taken of other earnings during the periods in the
summer when the steel plants are sometimes not in
operation. As has been said, many of the common
laborers go out on railway construction jobs. Some
of them, however, find work in other industries in
Granite City, particularly the Corn Products Refining
Company, which exceeded even its normal output during the period of depression — affording a significant
example of what diversity of industries means in a community.

The standard of living however is even more interesting. Among the Magyars, more of whom have
their women with them, the keeping of lodgers is well
nigh a universal custom. Out of forty-four families
studied, two-thirds kept lodgers. Of wives whose hus-
bands earned less than $400 a year nearly 74 per cent.
either worked or kept lodgers; but of those whose hus-
bands earned from $400 to $600 only 53 per cent.
worked or kept lodgers. But by far the larger number of Bulgarians live in groups, either on the " boarding boss " plan or under a system in which household
management is shared by the group.

The first plan is practiced by many Bulgarians and
Macedonians living in lodging houses, a couple of
rooms — one for sleeping and the other for cooking
— being rented by five or six men who employ a Ser-
vian, Austrian or Polish woman at a fixed amount per
month to do the buying, cooking, washing, and household work. The accounts for meat, groceries and

bread are kept under one name at the different stores, and at the end of the month each man pays his share of the aggregate expense.   Under the other plan the members of the group take turns in doing the cooking and housework, rent and cost of food being shared proportionately.   Each man, however, does his own washing unless the group, as in most cases, employs a woman to do it.

The crowding among these Bulgarian men is very great, the average number of persons in a room being 2.78 and the average per sleeping-room being 3.30. Of sleeping-rooms 22 per cent. have five or more persons, 48 per cent. have four or more, and 67 per cent. three or more.   According to one plant official, a tenement ordinance was once adopted establishing a minimum space for each sleeper.   Foreigners were dissatisfied, he said, and left the city in such numbers that the plants were crippled.   It became necessary to repeal the ordinance.

While doubtless other factors entered into the labor scarcity, one can readily believe that the Macedonian and Bulgarian lodging house proprietors were those mainly responsible for the dissatisfaction.   The monthly rent is about $1.11 per man.   The income which landlords derive from rent is " out of proportion to the investment, and excessive," says the report of the Immigration Commission.   The report continues:

By way of illustration, the cottages in " Hungary Hollow " may be considered.   These cottages usually have

three rooms, although some scattered here and there have
four rooms.   In each of these cottages twelve to sixteen
men live, paying a rent from $14 to $16 per month.   Mul-
tiplying these amounts by twelve to get the annual rents,
they are found to be $168 and $192 respectively.   These
rentals are the equivalent of an investment of $2,800 and
$3,200.   The original cost of the cottages, it is claimed,
was $1,500, although this seems to be an excessive esti-
mate.   On this basis, however, the landlords are receiving from 11 to 13 per cent. gross.   As the houses are
badly in need of repair, practically the only deduction to
be made is for taxes and insurance.   The cottages are
very similar to, but not so good as, those for which the
southern cotton mill operatives pay a rent of $3 to $3.50
per month.

As far as the rooming houses, which are conducted
by the mercantile establishments, are concerned, and in
which such a large proportion of the population lives,
the rents are from $5 to $8 per room.   Taking an average rental per room of $5, which is a very low esti-
mate, a mercantile house having fifty rooms to rent would
receive $250 in rentals per month, or $3,000 annually.
This amount represents the annual interest payment on
$50,000 at 6 per cent.   In practice a parallel case exists
to substantiate this supposition.   A mercantile house in
the community has fifty rooms for rent, from which it receives more than an average of $5 per room per month.
Its building cost $30,000.   The lower floor is occupied
by a saloon and two large stores.   The rental from its
rooms above the first floor, therefore pays over 10 per
cent. on the money invested in the entire building, or,
in other words, the income from the tenants pays more
than the ordinary rate of return on the cost of the build-

ing, and leaves free of rent the saloon and store-rooms, which are the most valuable part of the building for rental purposes.

From these illustrations, it seems clear that although the recent immigrant's per capita outgo for rent is small

MACEDONIAN LODGING HOUSE IN "HUNGARY HOLLOW"
These 45 rooms accommodate 200 lodgers

because he lives in a crowded condition, yet the rent he pays by groups or families is excessive and yields an unusually large rate of return to his landlord.

In the lodging houses owned and conducted by the "mercantile houses" as many as two hundred Bulgarians crowd into forty-five rooms during the full times of the winter when the steel mills are operating on their normal schedules. But the ordinary "mercantile company" conducts a varied business which often includes many such lines as grocery, meat market, dry goods and clothing shop, saloon, coffee house, bakery, bank, steamship agency, billiard-room, poolroom, amusement hall, real-estate and rental business, restaurant, and perhaps a weekly or semi-weekly newspaper.

The proprietors use their position to squeeze large profits out of their fellow-countrymen, but the average Bulgarian lives on so little that he is able to save much. This is shown by the fact that from one bank in Granite City no less than $50,000 was drawn in six weeks at the time of the Balkan War. In less than three hours one Sunday afternoon a meeting held in a dance pavilion contributed $4,600 to be sent to the Bulgarian Red Cross.

"Hungary Hollow," it should be stated, was not developed by the industrial plants or their realty companies, but by an independent real-estate company, to which several large unimproved tracts were sold. Although in turn it has sold much of the area to the foreigners it owns not a few of the houses where bad conditions obtain. This district is of course governed by the authorities of Granite City, of which it is a part, but they have neglected it shamefully. Until 1912 there was not a paved street and a year later but two. Sanitary supervision is conspicuous by its absence. One of the worst features is the dangerous grade crossing which separates the neighborhood from the

main part of Granite City.   Across a score of tracks,
carrying the freight and fast passenger trains of several trunk lines, every inhabitant of " Hungary Hollow " must go to reach the business center and most of
the industries of the city.   And the dwellers in the
central part of Granite City who work in the two or
three plants on the " Hungary Hollow " side of the

DANCE PAVILION IN " HUNGARY HOLLOW "

crossing have the same dangerous trip to make.   At
only one point is there a watchman.

Scarcely any of the denizens of the " Hollow " are
voters, and they have little to do with the civic affairs
of Granite City.   But over affairs among themselves
they have an interesting system of control which involves popular gatherings not unlike a town meeting.
It rests in the main on a " boss system " analogous to

that in our own city politics. The alien press has a large influence on public opinion, but the head of each "mercantile house," who in some instances is newspaper proprietor as well, is the most potent factor in the control of neighborhood affairs. He not only lodges many of his patrons but sells to all of them nearly everything they buy. And to him they look for advice in the affairs of life. He tells them of opportunities for work and advises them about accepting work which is offered.

So isolated are these Bulgarians from the American life beside and around them that an American almost thinks himself in a foreign country when he crosses the tracks. Visit "Hungary Hollow" in the latter part of May and you may find every doorway and window framed in green boughs brought in from the nearest woodland. On all sides you will hear singing and the music of the concertina, while every saloon and coffee house overflows with all sorts of festivity. You will be astonished to learn the occasion of it all: these comparatively uneducated foreigners are having a most hilarious time — and some of them are getting uproariously drunk — in honor of the origin of the Bulgarian alphabet and the two monks St. Methodius and St. Cyril, to whose credit that literary labor stands. During the Balkan War all such festivity as dancing and gay music was abandoned; national hymns and ballads descriptive of soldier life and bravery in death were mainly to be heard.

Just as "Hungary Hollow" has an important and

close relation with the workaday life of Granite City, so Granite City and the East Side are important parts of the St. Louis industrial district, and are increasingly recognized as such.   And just as " Hungary Hollow " shares scarcely at all in the civic and social activities of the city to which it belongs, so Granite City and the East Side are " out in the cold " so far as the civic plans and social progress of St. Louis are concerned. Of course, there is little initiative on the part of these communities to " join in."   And the inspiration which St. Louis extends to its western suburbs — identified with it in the same county and state governments — is entirely lacking in its relation to the East Side towns, whose volume of business and industrial output nevertheless it now gladly claims as swelling the greatness of the St. Louis district.

Naturally the broad river and the state boundaries break the identity of interests depending upon state, county or municipal legislation.   It is easy, therefore, to understand why a city plan for St. Louis and its environs has nothing to do with the region across the river, although it does not fail to present detailed schemes for the growth and improvement of areas much farther distant on the western side.   Yet arbitrary governmental boundaries of political units almost fade out in our modern conception of the " industrial district " and its development as a whole.   The essential social and civic unity of the same district should similarly be recognized.   Much might be gained through coöperating and coördinating action on the part of the several governmental authorities having jurisdiction in such a " district," and on the part of the volunteer social and civic agencies concerned.

The need for such harmonizing of effort is readily apparent in the St. Louis district. The St. Louis city infirmary and the relief societies are frequently imposed upon by applicants whose care is properly a responsibility of the Illinois communities. A wife deserter on either side can find refuge by merely crossing a bridge, and similarly criminals are glad to avail themselves of the state line as one additional barrier against pursuit, though the police of the two sides have some coöperative relations. Beggars come and go across the bridges, while the communities on either side make no attempt to dovetail their methods of handling this problem. Prostitutes when harassed on one side readily cross to the other. And the difference in the enforcement of Sunday closing laws is an open secret among the thirsty. Yet in the St. Louis Central Council of Social Agencies, comprising about fifty organizations, there is no representation from the East Side — due largely, no doubt, to the fact that there are few strong social agencies on that side of the river to be represented. But for the better handling of its own problems, if not to promote the social unity of the district, it would seem that St. Louis would do well to take greater interest in the encouragement of civic and social effort on the East Side.

Thus, while there is recognition of the industrial and commercial unity of the whole St. Louis " district," there is practically no expression of its real civic and social unity. This contrast is, of course, to be found in the relation of practically every large center of population to its industrial satellites. Yet here it seems to be even more sharply drawn than usual. The economic advantages of the East Side are, for certain industries, even more pronounced than is the case in the average suburban factory town; while the social and civic ties are even weaker. The East Side is valued for its industrial and commercial contributions to the district, and has the advice and help of the strongest St. Louis business organizations. But it is left to work out its own civic and social salvation.

What it has accomplished and what — through ignorance or apathy or preoccupation — it has failed to do, we have tried to outline briefly, using Granite City as a typical community.

We find a town planned, established and largely controlled by one industrial interest. Laid out in about the same unattractive fashion as other industrial towns of its class, it presents neither the showy front of some "model cities" nor the wretched conditions which are often to be found in family squalor behind such a mask. But its "Hungary Hollow," full of crowded and exploited Bulgarians, must not be forgotten.

Granite City is not a great deal above the American average of rather monotonous industrial communities. Few of its dwellings are of the worst sort, but none is of the attractive description which many English and a very few American industrial towns are providing. Exceptionally barren of resources for the social and recreational life of its inhabitants, it nevertheless seems to have little of the demoralization which usually accompanies such deficiencies. Founded in a paternalistic way, it has managed to avoid some of the worst mistakes of paternalism. Dominated by one industrial group, it has had neither spectacular " welfare " benefits, nor arbitrary regulation of everyday life in accordance with the whim of an autocrat priding himself on " his " men and what he does for them. Instead, there is a democratic spirit in the sharing of industrial power, as shown by the relations between employers and trade unions, which has worked out a more significant advance in industrial conditions — the substitution of the eight- for the twelve-hour shift in some steel processes, continuous and otherwise — than can be shown by other places where industrial autocracy is more pronounced.

CHAPTER VI

A CITY BY DECREE

MADE-TO-ORDER cities are the spectacular civic by-product of the new industrialism. Accustomed though Americans of this day are to rapid accomplishment, not one who visits the suddenly created city of Gary fails to experience a new thrill of amazement.

Gary is probably the greatest single calculated achievement of America's master industry. A score of steel towns have slowly grown from small beginnings. But the creators of Gary planned *de novo* a city which in five years attained a size equal to that acquired in thirty years of growth at Homestead. This made-to-order city is not unlikely to become the second city in Indiana before many decades pass.

Industrial power has perhaps never before had a simpler civic opportunity than when it brought in 1906 vast resources to an uninhabited wilderness at Lake Michigan's southern end. How did that power meet its civic responsibility, when there was nothing but a sand flat to gainsay its will, and how are the citizens meeting theirs now that the sand flat is a town? What of the relations between the two?

In April, 1906, the region was a waste of rolling sand dunes sparsely covered with scrub oak and interspersed with ponds and marshes. Three years later there was a great steel plant capable of employing 14,-000 men and covering approximately a square mile, equipped with a made-to-order harbor for the great ore freighters, and a town of 12,000 inhabitants, with fifteen miles of paved streets, twenty-five miles of cement sidewalks, two million dollars' worth of residences completed and occupied, a sewer system, water and gas plants, electric lighting, a national and a state bank, six hotels, three dailies and one weekly newspaper, two public schoolhouses, several substantial church edifices, ten denominations represented in church organizations, and many well-appointed stores and shops handling practically all the commodities that a good-sized city usually needs. There were 46 lawyers, 24 physicians and 6 dentists. And a thriving Commercial Club was aggressively boosting the town.

The federal census of 1910 found a population of 16,802. In November, 1912, there were more than 30,000, and in 1914 the number was estimated as high as 50,000. According to the report of the city officials for 1910 the building operations for that year involved $4,000,000. In 1914 the property valuation of the town reached $22,679,565 and the taxes raised for the fiscal year amounted to $400,000.

The average citizen scorns the thought that Gary is a " satellite " of Chicago if that implies dependence. The finger of unerring calculation, he tells you, has located the geographical spot where raw material can most economically be assembled and finished steel dis-

SITE OF GARY IN 1906

THREE YEARS LATER

tributed to the great Middle West markets. But it would appear that this advantage has been bound up in large part with Chicago's great railway facilities, all at Gary's service, with the Chicago labor market and with the housing accommodations of Chicago's southern suburbs. Furthermore the president and other principal officers of the subsidiary companies which have developed Gary are to be found in the heart of Chicago's business and financial district.

Room for efficient plant arrangement was undoubtedly one of the factors which led the shrewd and far-sighted men of the United States Steel Corporation to pour out a sum estimated at more than $75,000,000 to build plant, harbor and town.

Even these millions, spent " to clip a few vital seconds from the birth throes of a steel rail," as a recent writer has put it, are said to be only a half or a third of the total which will eventually be invested to place this new Pittsburgh on its level of maximum output.

The story of how the grouped steel plants have thus far been constructed; how it was actually cheaper to add to the site by filling in a part of Lake Michigan; how a river and a hundred miles of railroad track were incidentally shoved around so the site would fit; how the very plant arrangement spells economy; how the route from ore to finished steel has been straightened out to save delaying curves and reversals of direction; how thrift has banished smoke and its waste — giving the town a by-product of clear sky and clean air; how enormous power is gained from what were formerly the waste gases of blast furnaces; how " a thousand shortcuts " have been combined into tremendous saving : the story of all this is one to fascinate even the reader who has little scientific or economic interest.

The belief of the United States Steel Corporation in this new location for great industrial development is

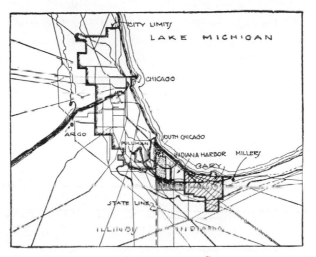

GARY IN RELATION TO CHICAGO

measured not alone by the great mills already at work. To assure space for the future, in which these mills may expand; to provide sites for many subsidiary manufacturing plants which make large use of steel; and to make some provision for the population of workers, a great tract of nearly twenty square miles was acquired, the shore frontage on Lake Michigan being eight consecutive miles, and the average width being two miles.

This tract was in a sense but a great addition to the corporation's already large holdings at South Chicago. All the plants except two occupy a strip between the Lake Michigan shore and the Grand Calumet River, which parallels it a mile or more to the south. The residential subdivisions laid out and developed by the Steel Corporation through its subsidiary, the Gary Land Company, occupy a strip flanking the south bank of the river. Still further south are the subdivisions which outside real-estate promoters are "booming." The Grand Calumet River separates all the plants, except one, from the town.

From east to west the industrial strip is given up to the hundreds of coke ovens which supply the gas needed in operating the steel mills; the possible site for a plant of the National Tube Company; the artificial harbor and the square mile of steel mills which flank it; the plant of the American Sheet and Tin Plate Company; the site for the proposed plant of the American Steel & Wire Company; the switch-yards and repair shops of the Elgin, Joliet & Eastern, the steel company's railroad; the site on which the American Car & Foundry Company will build and the plant of the American Bridge Company. This last is already second only to the Ambridge plant of the same company. When completed it will be the largest structural steel plant in the world.

That rank has already been obtained by another of

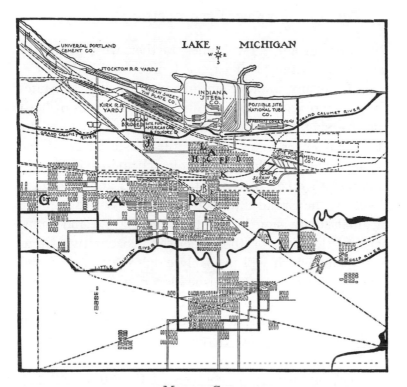

MAP OF GARY

The great steel mills occupy the area between the lake front and the Grand Calumet River. The town lies south of the river and its people have no convenient access to the Lake Michigan shore.

A. Grouping of Public Library, Y. M. C. A., and Post Office, on Fifth Avenue near Broadway.

B. Froebel school, with its park and recreation features, in the midst of a large population of poor foreigners.

C. Jefferson school, built by the company when the town was started.

D. Emerson school, a fine modern plant built by the public.

E. Neighborhood House, maintained by Presbyterians in the midst of a large foreign population.

F. City Hall.

G. Steel Company Hospital.

H. Mercy Hospital, under Catholic auspices, the money to build it raised, however, by a general-campaign committee of citizens with the Y. M. C. A. secretary as manager.

J. Housing development in connection with the plant of the American Bridge Company.

K. The first block in Gary's "patch" just south of the subdivision developed by the Gary Land Company. This block as it fronts on Broadway is a continuous row of saloons.

L. Concrete houses built for the employees of the American Sheet and Tin Plate Company.

P. P. Parks.

171

the Gary group.   Two miles farther west along the
lake shore is the plant of the Universal Portland Cement Company, another subsidiary of the United States
Steel Corporation.   It uses immense quantities of blast
furnace slag from the steel mills, and is operated by
electrical power generated by the waste gases of the
blast furnaces.   Thus the whole scheme of industries
is bound together with great adroitness and efficiency.
South of the Grand Calumet River and just east of the
original subdivision laid out by the Gary Land Company is the site for the American Locomotive Company plant which will probably employ 3,500 men and
have a capacity of fifty finished locomotives per month.
Near-by is the only one among all the plants not a direct subsidiary of the United States Steel Corporation
— the Gary Bolt and Screw Company, owned principally by Pittsburgh capital.

Gary's industry thus consists of the great mill and
the group of plants which use the steel it manufactures.

The contrast with the older plants and towns of the
Pittsburgh district is great.   There the steel industry
grew piecemeal by adding this part and that process
— its growth continually subject to the more or less
rigid conditions imposed by a long-established city.
The growth of the various plants was, in most cases,
not so rapid as to require any special housing provision
other than that which might unsystematically be supplied from time to time by the company or outsiders.
In some of the plants themselves, the installation of
larger and larger machinery and more extensive track-

age was not accompanied by any increase in the area covered. Under these conditions the leeway and "give" were wrenched from the human element. If tracks were needed in a passage-way previously used only by workmen afoot, the tracks came in, no additional passage-way being provided, and the workmen were obliged to dodge the shrieking little locomotives as best they could.

In Gary all is different. It was planned at the outset on an enormous scale. The visitor is impressed with the elbow-room, and the absence of dinginess and clutter such as characterize the average Pittsburgh steel mill. Men have light in which to see their work, room in which to do it, and an orderly arrangement that means as much for safety as any of the protection devices which have been installed.

So much for the industrial basis underlying Gary as a community. The conditions of work, the ever-increasing part played by machinery, the lessening of manual toil, the greater precision in handling material and directing processes, the better protection of the workman at his work — all the provision for his interplay of hand and mind with machine must here be left without further mention.

The unhampered opportunity to arrange the plants at Gary was equaled by the opportunity, likewise unhampered, to plan the streets, provide fundamental necessities for community life, determine the character of its houses, and predestine the lines of growth, all in the best and most enlightened way. The contrast between the arrangement and teamwork of the great plants and the rule-o'-thumb planning of Gary, the city, was pointed out in the first chapter.

The officials of the steel company say frankly that the building of the town was incidental, that their main concern was to construct a steel plant, and that city-making was a side issue into which only necessity drove them. They must have a place for their employees to live. This could not be expected to develop at all proportionately to the sudden need, unless the company assumed much of the responsibility.

They desired a healthy and efficient community to serve the daily life and needs of the men whose brains and muscle mean the real life of the plants.

The Gary Land Company, a subsidiary corporation of the United States Steel Corporation, was formed to secure the great tract of land to serve the present and long future needs of steel plant, town, and subsidiary manufacturing interests. Upon this company was thus thrown the task of making the town.

But it takes only a little inquiry to find out that the work of city building was given no such intelligent and forehanded consideration as should have been provided through the services of a professional city planning expert of the first caliber. It would appear, however, that some of the shortcomings at Gary have been recognized, for the development of the two latest steel towns, near Duluth and Detroit, shows considerable improvement.

The street plan of Gary is the old-fashioned rectangular gridiron. To anyone who has glanced even cursorily over a few of the two or three score city plan reports which have been made for American cities in the last decade, nothing is more evident than the effort to break up such rectangular street arrangement by diagonal direct routes. These can cut crosstown travel in two and add beauty and variety to the scheme of thoroughfares. It does not take much of a stretch of the imagination to see the future Gary employing a city planner whose report will propose belated diagonal streets cut at great expense through built-up sections.

With the steel plant foremost in mind, and the town incidental, the main fact in Gary's town plan is a wide street, Broadway, leading straight south from the mill entrance. Up this great artery in the morning and down it at night sweep the throngs of workers. But even with the mill gate as the focal point of the town, it is clear that diagonal streets leading southwest and southeast would be advantageous. Take only one of the many obvious instances. To go from the steel mill gate or from Broadway and Fifth Avenue, where important public buildings have been grouped, to the southwestern annexed part of Gary, one must travel approximately two miles covering two sides of a right angle. A direct diagonal would measure scarcely more than a mile and a half.

Many radical improvements could still be achieved at a cost very little greater than that involved in present haphazard lines of growth. The cost may be prohibitive later on.   The city has not as yet made good the corporation's short-sightedness.   Present requirements are merely that new streets shall be continuations of present streets and bear the same names.   Indeed the town has fallen back from some of the standards set by the industrial leaders.   The uniform building line which the Steel Corporation wisely stipulated in the subdivisions under its control has not been extended to other parts of the city.

In no way could the municipal officials of Gary render a more important service to their community, and incidentally go the steel corporation one better in making an orderly and beautiful city, than by bringing in expert city planners while yet there is plasticity. The Commercial Club of Gary has made a start in this direction by the appointment of a committee on city planning to work for boulevards, diagonal streets in outlying sections and the proposed lake front park. But the opportunity to grapple with a big situation in its formative stages should command ability of the first order.

It has already been pointed out that the plants occupy a strip along the lake front and that the steel companies set apart the strip adjoining it, òn the inland side, for residential purposes.   It was evidently their notion that the workmen in each plant would live back from it in a subdivision within walking distance of their work.   A principal thoroughfare was laid out parallel to the lake to connect all these subdivisions.   This is Fifth Avenue, eighty feet in width,

GARY STEEL MILL AND HARBOR

AT THE MILL GATE

with a grouping of public buildings on it at the point where Broadway one hundred feet wide, running south and inland from the main mill entrance, intersects it at right angles.

The town, however, has expanded quite as much to the south as along the flanks of the mills. Broadway is the main street to-day and has now been laid out six miles south from the mill entrance, and for well over three miles it is built up more or less continuously. Frequent street-car service for this distance has doubtless had much to do with its rapid development. City officials assert that this growth south of the steel company's residential strip was both unexpected and undesired by the company. The latter flatly denies this and says that it has consistently welcomed any growth or development of the city.

The expansion to the south not only calls for a reconsideration of the city structure but involves a situation both extraordinary and amusing. Gary's annexation experiences rival the most complicated matrimonial career that ever found its way into a divorce court. It seems that Indiana has a law permitting any town or city, by action of its board or council, to annex contiguous outside territory at any time. If it would avoid being summarily kidnaped, the contiguous territory must file in the proper court within thirty days a petition signed by two-thirds of all its voters. The burden of the situation is thus put, not on those who do the annexing, but on those who want to stay independent.

The " game " was started in the spring of 1910 when the city of East Chicago, Indiana, immediately west of Gary, suddenly embraced the larger city of Hammond which adjoins it on the far side. The councilmen of Gary, fearing that East Chicago in her thirst for dominion might without warning turn about and swallow up the future citadel of steel, decided as one city father declared to " beat her to it." Accordingly the mayor and the nine councilmen hastily met before daylight the very next morning and officially annexed the newly enlarged East Chicago.

Once started, Gary annexed the town of Tolleston, just to the southwest, and later the town of Miller just to the east. When these various places began to wake up to the situation a number of by no means uninteresting parleys resulted in a family understanding. East Chicago said she had not thought of wanting Gary and Gary acknowledged that the only reason she had annexed East Chicago was to prevent the reverse happening. Hammond put in her plea for single blessedness. So they all went to the superior court and agreed to disannex. Gary wanted to keep Tolleston and Miller, so they did not figure in these proceedings. Miller gained enough signatures to her petition to be allowed to go her own way. But Tolleston failed to do so and thus became a part of Gary, which thereby swelled to an area of thirty-two square miles.

One point should be especially noted in the layout of Gary. While it may fall short in its community fea-

tures, there are those who see in it an extraordinary
degree of industrial strategy. They spread before
you a map of the region and point out that the plants,
with Lake Michigan on the north, are separated from
the people on the south by the Grand Calumet River
which would thus serve as a veritable moat against
possible mob violence in times of stress. With the
lake front so extensively controlled by the company,
strike-breakers and supplies by the boatload from numerous ports on the Great Lakes could be brought
directly to the plants without risk. It is pointed out
that under such conditions a repetition of the Homestead strike would be impossible, and that perhaps no
great industrial plant or series of plants occupies a
position so impregnable to mob attack and so calculated to withstand a prolonged industrial siege.

Whatever the significance of this point may be, the
fact remains that the preoccupation of eight consecutive miles of the lake front for the plants has blocked
the chance of the community to secure an accessible
lake front park. The extent of the tract reserved for
industrial expansion is so great that even a roundabout
approach involves excessive distance and difficulty.

The economic importance of extensive harbor and
dockage facilities for the steel plant and all the subsidiary manufacturing interests should, of course, be
recognized. The region, however, is one of great
geological and botanical interest and its wild and distinctive scenery has for years attracted groups of
nature lovers from Chicago. From Chicago's stand-

point, therefore, it is desirable that regions of natural beauty near her boundaries be preserved for the use of the great and growing metropolitan population. But above all, it would seem that the needs of the future population of Gary might have been recognized at the outset. It was said that the steel companies "are not in the summer resort business," and that

BETWEEN STEEL MILL AND TOWN
Grand Calumet River. Steel Company's Office.

although the matter of the people's access to the lake was considered, it was not thought "safe for future industrial expansion" to set aside specific portions of shore for park purposes.

Two small parks, one two blocks in area and the other one block, were provided in the residential subdivision laid out by the Gary Land Company. One of these was early improved as a "beauty spot." The original knolls and trees had been left and grass was grown. But the conception of park function which was displayed may be gathered from the fact that although no part of the park was devoted to playground purposes, the pumping station and 500,000 gallon tower of the water works were placed on it. The concrete tower, however, presents a pleasing architectural effect.

The subdivision developed by the company flanks the steel mill on the south, with the Grand Calumet River between, as already indicated. Broadway, Fifth Avenue and the next parallel streets on either side of Broadway were reserved for business. Excepting Broadway and Fifth Avenue all streets are 60 feet in width. Along all streets but the four business streets a building line of 20, 25 or 35 feet is established. This has been observed in the building of company houses, and each contract for the sale of a lot stipulates its observance in any building to be erected. An alley, in most cases 30 feet wide, runs the long way in the center of each block. The lots in the residence districts are mostly 30 by 150 feet. A few are only 25 feet wide and the length of some is only 125 feet. It will be noted that this allows for a back yard, but that the space between houses is not likely to be considerable. Lots on the business streets are uniformly 125 feet in length. On Broadway and Fifth Avenue they are 25 feet wide; on the two other business streets paralleling Broadway they are 30 feet wide. The typical block is 600 feet in length with 40 lots of 30 feet width.

In the provision of the fundamental utilities to serve

the necessities of the population, efficiency and amplitude are manifest. With no permanent population yet on the ground and even before the streets were laid, the company immediately constructed sewer and water systems large enough for years to come. All sewers and water mains were laid in the alleys, so that in the future there would be little need of tearing up the streets to make repairs or new installation.

The cost of sewerage and paving was distributed over the lots in the subdivision, being included in the price of each so that there was no assessment for these improvements. The sewer system was so built that it could readily be extended to the subdivisions not owned and developed by the company, assessment on the lots defraying the cost.

Water supply is furnished by the Gary Heat, Light and Water Company, another subsidiary company of the steel corporation. It furnishes also, as its name implies, electric lighting and gas. For water supply a three-mile tunnel six feet in diameter extends a mile and a half into Lake Michigan. The capacity of the system is 20,000,000 gallons a day — enough for a population of 200,000.

To appreciate what an advance this meant over older steel towns, it may be recalled that, according to the Pittsburgh Survey, which studied other localities where the United States Steel Corporation has acted as landlord, Pittsburgh's "Painter's Row," inhabited by 568 people, for years had a single pump as the only supply of water fit to drink.

The housing provided by the corporation shows considerable diversity of architecture and little of the monotony ordinarily characteristic of "company housing." Solid rows of brick dwellings such as are

How Workers Lived in Construction Days
"Hunkies" abandoning their shack.

to be found at Pullman have been avoided   The 506 dwellings originally built by the Gary Land Company for the steel mill employees include:

50 frame houses, 4 rooms, renting at $12 to $13 a month

90 frame houses, 4, 5, and 6 rooms, renting at $14 to $20 a month

100 frame houses, 6 rooms, renting at $16.50 to $19.50 a month

266 brick, cement and timber houses, 5 to 10 rooms, renting at $23 to $42 a month

The Gary Land Company has also handled the housing provided by the American Bridge Company and the American Sheet and Tin Plate Company for the employees of their plants, though each of these companies made its own designs. Two miles west of Broadway is the new subdivision for the American Bridge Company houses. These include:

          1 nine-room house
          9 seven-room houses
         30 six-room houses
         30 five-room houses
         40 four-room houses
         72 five-room flats
        112 four-room flats

Each house or apartment has a bathroom additional. The company's experience in housing its employees at Ambridge, Pennsylvania, convinced it that such facilities were well used. It should be mentioned, however, that common laborers constitute not more than 30 per cent. of the working force.

The houses built by the sheet and tin plate company present an extensive experiment in the use of concrete. Particular interest attaches to them in view of Mr. Edison's enthusiastic predictions and the general impression that this is the coming method of supplying good housing at low cost for working people, especially when large numbers of houses are built at the same time and place. With the largest cement works in the country at Gary, operated as a subsidiary of the steel corporation, it may seem strange that concrete construction was not attempted at the beginning of the town. The reason put forward is that the need for houses was so pressing as not to warrant the risk involved in experimentation.

The sheet and tin plate company decided to take the risk. Many points of superiority are claimed for concrete houses. They are indestructible, thus reducing fire risk to the minimum. They are sanitary, to an extent impossible to obtain in the ordinary frame or brick house. Deterioration is so slight as to reduce repair bills and maintenance costs to the lowest figure. And the cost, according to those responsible for the development at Gary, is not expected to exceed the cost of fairly well-built frame houses.

From the capitalist's point of view it is urged that a concrete house is a far better investment at 8 per cent. than a frame house is at 10 per cent.

Curiously enough the actual decision to use concrete construction came when the sheet and tin plate company's engineer found excessively high building costs at Gary, due to high wage scales established by the building trade unions. It became necessary to devise a construction scheme which, by the use of machinery, would reduce the labor factor to the smallest proportions. This led in turn to the design and construction of special machinery and adaptable molds. With this initial cost out of the way, the company can build additional houses at a still lower cost.

The first group of houses consists of:

24 apartments, some of 3 rooms at $12.50 a month
    but mostly of 4 rooms   at 16.00 a month
40 five-room houses   at 17.50 a month
30 six-room houses   at 20.00 a month
10 nine-room houses (3 stories) at 27.50 a month
 6 detached houses.

Most of these houses are in terrace construction in groups of six or ten. Each house or apartment has a bathroom, pantry, and a coal bunker under the front porch.

CONCRETE HOUSES AT GARY

Sheet and tin plate company employees eagerly rented the whole supply, finding the rentals considerably cheaper than corresponding accommodations elsewhere in the town. The tenants are all skilled workmen, mainly American.

Experience with the concrete houses has thus far not measured up to the highest hopes entertained at the outset. But it is perhaps still too soon to pass final judgment on the experiment.

Under the Gary Land Company's terms of sale, referred to in the first chapter, the sale price, according to the statement of the superintendent, covers the actual cost of the land, the cost of the complete improvements — street paving, sidewalks, sewers, etc., and the cost of the house plus 5 per cent. per year. The total amount may be paid in ten annual installments, with 5 per cent. interest on deferred payments. This amounts to very little more than rent. If the householder is discharged, or voluntarily quits work, or for any reason wants to anticipate his payments, he can do so. Or if he wants to turn back his house, the amount he has paid in will be refunded, minus 9 per cent. a year as rent. In case of his death similar terms are open to his heirs. American Bridge Company officials declare that such a scheme has proved satisfactory at Ambridge. By distribution of seeds and free water for garden purposes, the Gary Land Company has made efforts to encourage tenants to keep their premises attractive. It has offered prizes for the best lawns and has planted several thousand trees.

The agreement concerning the sale of a lot stipulates that the plans must be approved by the agent of the company, that the building must be completed within eighteen months, that it must be built back of the prescribed building line, and that no liquor is ever to be sold on the premises. Exception to the latter provision was made in the case of a few places on Broadway.

The company has from the beginning sought to sell its houses and lots as rapidly as possible to the steel workers. It has kept its prices below those asked for many of the less advantageously located lots outside of its subdivisions, and it has used care to see that its houses and lots have not fallen into the hands of speculators planning to gain handsome profits by re-selling to the workers.

Housing provision by the company for low-paid un-skilled labor has been unsatisfactory and inadequate in Gary as in other towns of the Steel Corporation. In fact, the industrial captains have scarcely made any real effort to solve the problem. In the early days construction workers, several thousand in number, were largely left to provide themselves with shelter. Tents and shacks, contraptions of boards, tar paper, canvas, tin, and anything else at hand, sprang up like weeds. And with a little banking of sand against their walls as a feeble protection against winter cold, they served as habitation for immigrant laborers through many months. Even some of the better com-pany efforts were not much of an improvement.

When the American Bridge Company was erecting its plant the huts which were provided bunked thirty or forty men in a room not only too small but poorly ventilated and lighted. The men were left to do their own cooking, with no facilities except crude fireplaces, which they built of stones and pieces of corrugated iron around the hut entrances. Construction workers have been known to pack themselves to the number of thirty-five in a one-room shanty thirty by fifteen feet, half of them sleeping by day and half by night. Each man merely had a blanket in which he rolled up on his allotted floor space. The windows were never open and a Gary physician states that among the thirty-five men he found six cases of tuberculosis.

For the permanent unskilled work force two groups of houses were built when the company's first subdivision was developed. These were in Kirkville in the northwestern corner and in " Hunkyville " in the northeastern corner. The experience was somewhat dismal with the problems of dirt and rural habits among those foreigners who take in an indefinite num ber of boarders. Miss Byington's study of the boarding boss establishments in Homestead [1] and Mr. W. Jett Lauck's analysis [2] of wages, rents and overcrowding at Granite City, show that the unskilled laborer with a family looks to the lodger as the often necessary means for supplementing wages.

Even " Hunkyville's " four rows of " double dry goods boxes "— four rooms and a bath-tub to each house — were a height of civilization, the complexities of which were not entirely comprehensible to the dwellers. The sanitary conveniences were particularly misunderstood. It was a common impression, according to the company, that something must be out of order if the water ever stopped running from a faucet

[1] See " Homestead : The Households of a Mill Town," by Margaret F. Byington, Survey Associates.
[2] Pp. 152 ff.

"Hunkyville"

In Gary's Best Residential Section

or in any appliance. Education was reduced at once to terms of economics. It was found that the water bill in a single " Hunkyville " dwelling sometimes amounted to as much as $11.50 a month. That of the largest house in Gary, occupied by the mill superintendent, rarely reached $2. Inspectors from the water office had little difficulty in teaching the man on wages of $1.60 a day how to use water without running up a bill of $11.50 a month. The crowding in these cheapest grade houses was almost as bad as that in some of the shacks. Thirty-eight of the four-room dwellings — 142 rooms — at one time contained 428 people.

Flagrant abuses of the property by the tenants are instanced by the company. It despaired of its efforts to teach better ways of living, and rather than be responsible for the miserably insanitary conditions which prevailed, it ordered the tenants of " Hunky-ville " to move out. The houses were then put in order for American and foreign workingmen with families, who agreed not to crowd their houses with boarders.

The complete failure of the company to work out the housing needs of its low-paid immigrant labor was emphasized by its apparent indifference as to where the " hunkies " found a new abode. It was glad to continue to utilize their muscle in the mill, but it no longer cared to concern itself with providing their homes or educating them to American standards of living. Practically the only place for them to go was Gary's " south side." This part of the town lies outside of the company's subdivisions. It has been developed largely by real-estate speculators and contains the worst and most menacing of housing conditions, as the next chapter will point out. The growth of these conditions and the outrageous exploitation of the workers by greedy landlords and real-estate companies found no effective opposition from the industrial power, responsible for the creation of the city.

The failure of the company to protect its workers from such exploitation, as might have been done through adequate provision of housing for its lowest grade of labor, is on the other hand paralleled by the effort of a group of men connected with the steel company to saddle a blanket fifty-year trolley franchise on the community. How the citizens dealt with this forms part of the human story of Gary.

Into the made-to-order city came the people — workmen, wives and children, mill officials, shop-keepers, bankers, lawyers, ministers, doctors, school teachers, newspaper men. Then arose public spirit and private greed, and all the other human elements which mingle in the body politic. The city created by fiat found its destinies now delivered into the hands of the human beings for whom it was fashioned. How they fitted into the framework, how the structure of community organization grew, how townspeople and industrial authority have managed together — all this marks the emergence of democracy in a city created by decree.

CHAPTER VII

THE EMERGENCE OF DEMOCRACY

" IF you'll give us the colors we want, Sophie will do the painting herself." This, broken up into foreign-sounding English, ended the parley with the company decorator. He was putting a new coat on the interiors of houses provided for the cheapest immigrant labor of the steel mill.

But " Hunkyville," as this section was dubbed by the rest of the town, had a little school girl who, unabashed, challenged the United States Steel Corporation's scheme of art. And in the " box " occupied by her family she had her way. Outside it remained like all the rest in the row, but indoors, with stencil designs, such as she had learned to make at school, she painted the walls with borders at the top and panels running down to the floor.

This episode tells the human story of Gary — wholesale provision for community life, and that life itself surging in to cut its own channel for expression.

The inhabitants are mainly, of course, the working force of the steel mill and the subsidiary plants — officials, foremen, American and foreign skilled workingmen, and the unskilled laborers, nearly all foreign. But civic affairs have been influenced quite as much

194

by the smaller number of men not identified with the Steel Corporation.   One of them was early elected as mayor.   To   this   element — real-estate   operators, tradesmen, and all sorts of foot-loose incomers, anxious to try their fortune in a place that offers quick development — is attributable much of the pioneer spirit that reminds one of the Far West.

In fact, the early conditions of the place, just twenty-six miles from downtown Chicago, were startingly like those of a frontier town.   The region had its traditions.   The sand dunes three years before had been the scene of pitched battles between the Chicago police and the notorious " car barn bandits " who were eventually captured and hung.   And the earliest construction crews had their quota of ruffians.   Like a new mining   camp,   Gary   attracted   adventurers   whose " pasts," even if known, mattered little to a community absorbed in the here and now.

With such a mixture of people it is not surprising that the civic history of Gary has packed into a few short years all the political intrigue and struggle, the " gang rule," the " graft exposures " and " reform movements " which usually occupy a generation.   Her first mayor, owing to the bitterness of the strife, was arrested no less than fourteen times in a period of two years without having a charge proved against him in court.   But her citizenship has shown an independent spirit especially in relation to the industrial power.

In the growth of Gary's population the first stage was that of the construction workers.   Describing their sudden influx, to the number of 6,000, an "oldest inhabitant" who had arrived in 1906, said it seemed as if people just "sprouted out of the ground." This construction force was brought in mainly by contractors. With the coming of the permanent force of employees for the steel mill, the proportion of skilled workers increased. But many of the construction laborers remained, for some of them found places in the mill and others were needed in further construction work in connection with the plants of subsidiary companies of the steel corporation.

At the start there were barely enough voters to organize a town government. Gary's vote in April, 1907, was 29; in November, 1908, it was over 2,000; and in November, 1912, it was 4,537. In November, 1908, a rough census taken by the Gary Land Company showed a polyglot population as follows:

Slavonians	300
Hungarians	325
Croatians	950
Bohemians	125
Servians	1,000
Montenegrans	375
Turks	40
Macedonians	100
Armenians	25
Greeks	40
Russians	150
Poles (German and Russian)	1,100
Germans	150

Belgians	15
French	6
Norwegians	75
Swedes	125
Danes	15
Finns	20
Italians	350
Japanese	10
Negroes	250
Welsh	50
Jews	150
Irish, Scotch, English, Canadians and Americans	4,500
	10,246

Of these 10,246 people it was estimated that between 5,000 and 7,000 were men of voting age. The " foreigners "— those not Americans, English, Scotch, Irish or Canadians, were about 56 per cent. A similar rough census made in 1912, placed the number of such " foreigners " at 12,000 in a total population of 30,000, or about 40 per cent.

With rapid community growth assured by the big plants under construction and the inpouring of people, the early days of Gary witnessed a scramble for the " ground floor " advantages which the future might magnify. Shrewd real-estate speculators at once saw their opportunity in the lack of adequate company housing for the foreigners and they seized upon land south of the company subdivisions. The wretched housing conditions which developed on Gary's " south side " were and still are a disgrace to the industrial power which created the town, to the town authorities and to the state of Indiana.

The prices which workers on low wages were inveigled into paying the speculators amounted practically to robbery.   To illustrate: a foreigner was induced to pay $1,800 for two lots adjacent to two others which were bought for $700 by persons who knew actual land values.   The payment of installments on outrageous land contracts is a hard and unnecessary burden on many a struggling Gary family, and has pitifully limited the sum available for house-building.   Speculative builders put up flimsy, box-like frame houses by the hundreds.   Even so the scarcity of housing accommodations has made exorbitant rents possible.

The most flagrant examples in all this bad housing are to be found in a score or more of barrack-like shacks to which the former denizens of " Hunkyville," ousted by the company, had to turn.   A typical shack is about 18 feet wide, 100 long, and one low story in height.   The little space at the end of a 125-foot lot is occupied by the privies, one for every two " apartments."   When two of these shacks are on adjoining lots, there is scarcely more than three feet between them.   Standing on posts a couple of feet above the ground, the structure is built solely of boards, outside walls as well as partitions.

An " apartment " extends across the width, each of the two rooms thus measuring about nine by nine feet.

The room on one side of the building has a door and a window; the other room, two windows.   There is no running water and one pump usually serves all the people in an entire shack or perhaps two.   Slops and the less bulky refuse are merely thrown out of the door of the apartment into the unpaved passage-way.   Two typical shacks, separated by a narrow passage-way into which the doors of the " apartments " opened, còn-

REAL-ESTATE EXPLOITATION OF WORKERS
These "apartments," housing eight families and many boarders,
yield excessive profits.

tained eight apartments each, two of the sixteen being unoccupied.   In the twenty-eight rooms no less than sixty people lived.   In most cases the family has two or three boarders additional; and not infrequently one finds a group of single men keeping house — such as it is — by themselves.

Two-room " apartments " rented for $6 to $9 a month.   The average would certainly not be lower than $7.50.   One shack contained seven apartments at this figure, and a small space at the end which was rented as a saloon at $35 a month. When wholly occupied, the monthly rental would thus total $87.50, and amount to $1,050 in a year. At a liberal estimate the construction of the shack could not have exceeded $1,-700 and the cost of the lot $500. On the total of this investment, therefore, the income was approximately 50 per cent. a year. Even if some of the space was for varying periods unoccupied, the return would certainly be " good."

Another shack, containing eight apartments, renting at $6 apiece, cost, according to the owner's statement, about $1,600; a contractor stated that he would be glad to build one like it for $1,450, and another estimate was still lower. With all the apartments filled, the total rental per year would be $575. In both of these typical cases no account has been taken of the amounts the tenants charged their boarders.

The building of such shacks, as well as of the ramshackle hovels of boards, tin and tar-paper, some of which still exist as a remnant of the early days, is now fortunately prohibited in Gary, but they are sufficiently substantial to remain a serious problem for some time to come.

Nor is overcrowding confined to the shacks. Such cases may be found as that of a man with a wife and baby who rents a six-room flat at $45 a month and sublets three of the rooms to lodgers, his own family using the kitchen, and even the bathroom sometimes, for sleeping purposes. In the ordinary four-room houses in Kirkville or throughout the south side the immigrant family which does not have boarders is an exception. Typical four-room households are: a couple with two children and five boarders — nine altogether; a man and his wife and ten boarders; a man and his wife and eight boarders. The head of the Presbyterian Neighborhood House settlement vouched for one case of a Ruthenian and his wife and twenty-five boarders, all in seven rooms. The man did the cooking and prepared the lunch baskets.

A few of Gary's more public-spirited people feel the reproach which these conditions reflect on her civic life. Not many share the point of view of one owner who, when asked if the city authorities were requiring better conditions in the shacks, said: " Yes, they even want us to put in running water, but a rail pen is good enough for ' hunkies.' " In unconscious irony he placarded his barracks with the sign of the " Indiana Improvement Company."

Gary's building regulations have been inadequate from the first, and her building commissioner at the time of the writer's visit to the town showed little grasp of the situation — in fact was scarcely aware of any " problem." The regulations contained practically nothing to prevent some of the conditions which have led to the worst slums in other cities. There was not a word about windowless rooms, minimum requirements of air space in bedrooms, use of basements for living purposes, etc. Small shafts for light and air were stipulated but the proportion of lot area which

might be covered by houses was absolutely unrestricted.

The commissioner even volunteered the information
that when a cheap house was to be built he urged that
it be placed on the rear of the lot. A premium was
thus put on the building of two houses on a single lot.
What this means could be learned by a visit to the tenement districts of a city like Chicago.

The Indiana housing law was passed in 1909 and at
first applied only to the two largest cities in the state,
Indianapolis and Evansville. Not until 1913, was it
extended so as to cover Gary. Its provisions preclude
many of the evils so rampant in the housing development prior to 1913. But it is one more case of the
stable door being locked after a great many horses had
been stolen. Furthermore, the state law applies only
to tenements. It forbids one tenement back of another
on the same lot. But only the local ordinances can
forbid the building of single houses in the rear of
front tenements.

It is not a minute too soon for Gary to begin to
" head off the slum " by the adoption of a stricter
municipal housing code. Aggressive selfishness of the
real-estate speculators, given free rein by popular ignorance and indifference, is still operating to fasten on
northern Indiana the worst of Chicago conditions.
These are spreading from South Chicago through the
string of industrial towns stretching eastward to Gary.
As they all grow together and push further eastward,
the workers for civic improvement in Indiana fear that

the result will be a belt of dreary housing on twenty-five-foot lots clear across the State.

Living costs in Gary, while at their highest in rents, are by no means low in other necessities. A comparison of food prices at two stores in Gary and at an average store in Chicago showed that the Gary rates were never less, and almost always more, than those charged in Chicago. Moreover, an investigator who inquired the prices at the Gary stores and then examined the grocery books found in the homes frequently discovered discrepancies, which were always to the advantage of the store. Several household budgets were secured. Those of two Polish households, the one of a family group, the other of a boarding boss establishment, throw light on the housing conditions already discussed.

Family " A "— Polish — consists of six: man, wife, wife's brother, three children under seven. Expenses per month: Rent $7.50; food $37.50; fuel averages $4.51 ($5.42 in winter and $3.60 in summer); clothes $2; tobacco and beer $1.35; doctor $6.00. Even with the absurdly low estimate for clothing — the wife said the man bought one second-hand suit a year, and that she sewed all the other clothing by hand — the budget amounts to $58.36 a month. The head of the family earns $2 a day in the steel mill.

Family " B "— Polish — consists of man, wife and ten lodgers. Expenses for month: Rent $17; food $62.46; fuel $5.42; clothing $5; furniture $5; water rate $.75. Total $95.63. The man earns $1.43 a day, amounting to about $40 a month. The ten lodgers pay a total of about $90 a month, or more than double the man's earnings.

Three charity visitors, a settlement resident and a visiting nurse estimated that in South Chicago the cost of securing for one year the bare decencies of life for a family of five amounts to $630. In Gary this figure would be swelled considerably by higher rent and food costs. The wage scales at the Gary steel mills are the same as at South Chicago, and the problem at Gary of making both ends meet must be even more acute than at South Chicago, where as John A. Fitch [1] shows, the common laborer, at seventeen and one-half cents an hour, cannot earn this minimum in three hundred days of twelve hours each, nor in three hundred and sixty-five days of ten hours each. It is, of course, pointed out that many low-paid immigrant workingmen have hundreds of dollars in the banks at Gary. This may be accounted for in part by the large numbers of single men. And anyone familiar with foreign colonies knows that many families, also, are satisfied with the lowest standard of living in order to save. A family which desires normal home life cannot economize by spending less than enough for physical efficiency. Neither can it solve its problem if it jeopardizes its children's well-being.

There are undoubtedly some cases of what amounts to actual polyandry in Gary. A doctor of established position in the community is authority for the statement that ten boarders who lived with a couple habitually had relations with the wife, all with the entire

[1] See "The Labor Policies of Unrestricted Capital," by John A. Fitch. *The Survey*, April 6, 1912, p. 19.

knowledge and consent of the husband.   How prevalent such conditions may be, it is difficult to say, but one
well-informed citizen expressed his belief that many
of the boarding foreigners live in such a way that
relations with the woman of the household are taken
as a matter of course along with board and lodging.

Despite the poor housing and insanitary conditions
of the " south side " Gary has not yet been menaced by
any serious epidemic of infectious diseases.   Climate,
sandy soil, excellent water supply are important health
factors.   The water system is being extended throughout the city, displacing the many wells.

As the sewers also are developed, the dangers which
now lurk in the privies and the indiscriminate disposal
of slops ought to diminish.   Some effort has been
made to keep wells and privies reasonably far apart,
but there are many evil conditions throughout large
sections of the south side which could be eliminated
under the state law making it "unlawful for any
person, firm, company or corporation to institute, permit or maintain any conditions whatever which may
transmit, generate, or promote disease."

Although the health department is said to have
greatly increased in efficiency recently, the city for
years has not appropriated funds sufficient to support
an up-to-date health administration.   A recent city report shows that in one year it paid $1,837.55 to preserve
its health, $25,084.41 to keep itself from burning up,
and $33,583.26 to get itself arrested.   One difficulty is
a state law which limits the salaries of health officers.

The rough-and-ready methods of safeguarding health in the early days at one time necessitated wholesale vaccination. A picturesque description tells how smallpox broke out in a crowd of negroes who were promptly quarantined, a " pest house in the bush " being hastily established. Immediately a force of physicians was hurried into the town to vaccinate the whole population. The process was a strange one to the " hunkies " and explanation was too laborious and slow. They fled in terror whenever approached, so that a common sight on Broadway was a " hunky " tearing down the street pursued by a policeman and a doctor — satchel in hand. The captured victim was at once pinned to the curbstone or pavement, his leg or arm bared, and despite sputtering protestations the job was triumphantly performed.

Under the health department at the time of the writer's personal observation, one deputy health officer was charged with the inspection of food and its handling, including the dairies supplying milk. An excellent and obviously well-enforced regulation prohibited the display of goods on the sidewalks. Another deputy, a woman, devoted attention to insanitary living conditions. Although not possessed of much technical knowledge, she was active in dealing with obvious evils. Not only premises, but bad conditions inside the houses, even the care of babies, received her attention. In a small way, moreover, she brought various agencies to bear upon cases of dire poverty.

Diseases due to poor nourishment or bad air were

frequent, according to one of the health officials. The city had its full share of tuberculosis and pneumonia, and these diseases, he believed, were fostered by the fact that many men came from hours of work in a highly heated atmosphere into cold air and then breathed the foul air of the shacks.

The three health commissioners took turns in serving as executive of the board. One of them, whose training and professional record had been the subject of criticism, was more active than many another man of greater learning. Through newspaper publicity and talks on hygiene to the school children he kept the subject of health before the people. But both his ability and his singleness of purpose were questioned by men who declare that his main object was to increase his private practice and his political prestige. One of his deputies habitually distributed the health commissioner's personal card, suggesting him as a good doctor to go to in case of illness. In response to a question concerning the milk supply, this deputy made the naïve reply that " the man brings it around "— an index of the inefficiency which characterized much of the health administration at that time. One of the greatest recent advances in Gary has been the more effective work of the health department, under a new city administration, though it has thus far failed to grapple with the housing conditions.

Saloons have given Gary a distinction of which the better citizens are not proud. In April, 1911, there were 238 to about 21,000 population. It is doubtful

if another city of that size in the United States had so
many.   Margaret F. Byington [1] reports that in Homestead, a city of 25,000 people, there were at the time
of her investigation sixty-five saloons, ten wholesale
liquor stores, a number of beer agents, innumerable
" speakeasies " and a dozen or more " drug-stores."
Even if we totaled this assortment as a round hundred
saloons, the proportion would be one saloon to every
250 people, whereas the proportion in Gary was one
saloon to about every 88 people.

A typical working people's ward in Chicago has 304
saloons in a total population of 70,099 — a proportion
of one saloon to every 231 people.   The McKeesport
saloon-keeper, instanced by John A. Fitch,[2] who started
in without a cent and became a retired capitalist in
four years is matched in the case of a young Italian in
Gary who, starting similarly, soon reached the $30,000
mark and took a trip to Europe to celebrate.

Gary started as a " wet " city, except that in the first
subdivision the company stipulated in every contract
for the sale of a lot that the premises should not be
used for the sale of liquor.   In only two places in this
subdivision did it permit bars.   Early in 1908 a petition was signed by a sufficient number of voters at the
previous general election, though a comparatively small
proportion of all the voters in the city at the time of
the petition, to prevent for two years the granting of

[1] *See* "Homestead," by Margaret F. Byington, a volume in the
Pittsburgh Survey, p. 27.
[2] *See* article in *The Survey* for March 6, 1909.

additional saloon licenses. When this more or less dry period came to an end, the rush to establish saloons rivaled that of a gold excitement.

In the spring of 1911, however, Indiana passed a law under which Gary saloon licenses rose from $375 to $725 each, of which amount $500 goes to the city, $200 to the state, and $25 to the federal government. Another provision of the same state law specifies that no new licenses shall be granted until the proportion of one saloon to every 500 people is reached. If the present 172 saloons are now paying businesses, they should reap large profits as the city rapidly grows.

There are many contrasts between Gary as a work town controlled by the steel industry and Gary as a community which is being developed by the people of the place. One of these contrasts involves labor organization. Trade unions have been alert to the significance of any success they may attain in a town created by a corporation which has so conspicuously fought labor organization. The American Federation of Labor in March, 1910, presented to President Taft bitter charges against conditions in the Gary plants.

The efforts to organize the mills have not succeeded; but the crying need of the town for more houses gave the building trades a foothold. The very fact that in 1910-1911 jurisdictional disputes among these unions nearly put a stop to all building operations indicates the extent to which they had taken lodgment. So critical did this become that the Commercial Club of Gary appointed a committee and went to great pains in its efforts to adjust the difficulties.

Evidences of what these organizations have accomplished for their members are bound to impress the steel workers. Ignorance of the English language is a barrier, but even the immigrant laborers in the steel mill who earn 17½ cents an hour cannot fail some day to wake up to the fact that laborers doing similar work in Gary building operations are paid from 34 to 37 cents an hour. The demand at times for labor has indeed drawn not a few "hunkies" from the steel mill to the better pay in the town.

Intermittency of work has at times been a serious problem. For several months, beginning in the fall of 1910, the steel mill was operated at only about 40 per cent. of its full capacity. The unemployed included some who go from one point to another hunting jobs. One recent arrival from Westmoreland County, Pennsylvania, was still considerably preoccupied by the dangers of a region where "they shoots men."

The independent spirit of the citizens which cropped out early in connection with the trolley franchise, has been felt since the beginning in the local politics and has reached its highest positive expression in the development of the school system.

A group of men connected with the steel company, sought but failed to secure the trolley franchise. Their proposition was for exclusive rights for fifty years, covering all existing streets and alleys, including any subsequent extensions, with authorization to charge a flat five-cent fare. The terms granted to a rival company, which is now operating, although of fifty years' duration, stipulate the following: only certain streets to be used; company to pave 26 feet of the width of such streets; at the expiration of five years tickets to be sold at the rate of eight for 25 cents, but six to be sold for 25 cents from the beginning (the company anticipated its contract by furnishing eight tickets for 25 cents for use during the four hours a day in which laboring men go to and return from work); interurban railroads coming from a greater distance than five miles to be furnished with power and the use of the company's tracks at a rate not to exceed two cents per passenger, an arbitration plan being provided in case this rate is thought to be exorbitant.

How there could be any difference of opinion among the citizens as to which franchise to choose is a mystery. That a fifty-year grant under any circumstances to any company was even considered by an up-to-date citizenship is extraordinary, in view of the public attention which has been directed to the struggles of the larger cities against such long-term grants.

The Gary Heat, Light and Water Company, a subsidiary of the Steel Corporation, supplies gas, electricity and water, having a twenty-five-year franchise under which the city can buy the plant at its then value. The gas rate was $1.10 per thousand, with a discount of 10 per cent. for payment within ten days, bringing it down to $1. The company claims that it seeks only a reasonable return on its investment, and is primarily seeking to give good service to the town. On July 1, 1912, it voluntarily reduced the price of gas to $1, with a discount of ten cents if bills are paid in ten days.

Electricity was furnished at eleven cents per kilowatt hour, with 10 per cent. discount for payment within ten days, though users of large quantities could secure it at a lower cost. These rates were reduced 20 per cent. on July 1, 1912. The charge for water was thirty cents per thousand gallons, reduced July 1, 1912, to twenty-five cents. This rate is varied according to quantity used and certain other factors. For instance, in the poorer houses, where there is but one faucet, a flat rate of eight dollars a year obtains. The rate of thirty cents per thousand seems high when it is known that at Hammond, a few miles west, a municipal plant supplied it at seven cents. The quality, however, is generally acknowledged to be far superior at Gary, and the plant, involving a large investment, has a capacity to serve the future needs of a quarter of a million people. Public regulation of rates is not provided for in these franchises, and must come, if at all, through whatever procedure the general laws of Indiana permit.

If the fight against the trolley franchise sought by the steel company group aroused antagonisms, the struggles in local politics have generated even greater bitterness. If you were to believe all the sensational accounts which appeared a few years ago in newspapers the country over, you would think that at one period of its political history, the entire voting population of the steel city celebrated election day by getting arrested. The pioneer spirit of the place probably found its readiest expression in the political turbulence.

One factor productive of sudden shiftings is the easy naturalization possible under Indiana laws. The large number of foreign voters, beset here, as in Pittsburgh, by the old cry that a protective tariff means good times in the steel industry, have in national elections usually given the Republican party a substantial margin. The story is told that a group of " hunkies " who did not understand very much English came into a restaurant. The waiter asked for their orders. They all promptly repeated their leader's reply of " Taft." But in 1912 the Progressive party triumphed by a vote of 1,815 for Roosevelt, as compared with 1,286 for Wilson, 1,083 for Taft, 320 for Debs, and 33 for Chapin.

While in municipal issues the Democrats were always victorious until a Fusion ticket defeated them in November, 1913, the county, on the other hand, has usually gone Republican. This situation gave to each side some local authority which was invariably exercised at election time. The Democratic city administration always controlled the police force and swore in a lot of special officers. Similarly, the Republican sheriff appointed a large number of special deputies. Whenever some disturbance arose at a polling place, a wagon load of special policemen and another wagon load of deputy sheriffs arrived on the scene; the disturbance, instead of subsiding, often increased in violence.

The city's political strife has centered around one picturesque personality. For the issue has much of the time been Knotts *versus* anti-Knotts. At one time a school teacher, at another Indian agent among the Sioux, later insurance man, " Tom " Knotts had served as a police commissioner of Hammond and as president of the town board of Gary, when, in 1909, he was elected at Gary's first city election for a four-year term as mayor. Despite the fact that the mayor was arrested fourteen times in two years, despite graft " exposures " and much bitterness, there are not many citizens who express a downright distrust in the man who served so long as their chief executive. On the whole, most people give him credit for a very real desire to do the best thing for the interests of the city.

As Knotts himself put it, " We [meaning the town board] were just three bushwhackers and we had to learn how to manage public affairs as we went along." In forming an opinion of the efficiency of his administration, some of the handicaps under which it labored must be weighed. The mayor had to contend with a " combine " against him in councils. The extraordinary number of saloons may perhaps account for the fact, which is none the less significant, that for a considerable period six of the nine councilmen — one from each of six wards and three at large — were saloon-keepers, some of them most disreputable.

The graft " exposure " which was widely heralded

to the nation did not make good.   A man from Louisville wanted a franchise for a heat supply company. He claims that he found it necessary to bribe the mayor, the city engineer and several aldermen.   By means of a dictagraph he reported the guilty conversations with the latter.   But the mayor was made a more spectacular culprit by the " discovery " of $5,000 in marked bills in his desk.   He claims that they were put there by men who wanted to trap him, and it must be said that the charge was never proven.

One alderman was convicted, but never served his term, since he died pending the appeal of his case.   The jury disagreed in the case of the city engineer.   But the prosecution in general was upset by the declaration of the dictagraph stenographer that, at the direction of the Louisville man, he " fixed up " the report of the bribery conversation.   And then the former city clerk, whose testimony had been damaging to the alderman later convicted, disappeared and sent a deposition that his testimony was perjured.   The whole prosecution was then abandoned.   Recently the former city clerk turned up and announced that the deposition was forced from him at the point of a revolver and under threat that his previous prison record would be exposed. Most citizens who are not bitterly partisan in Gary politics are inclined to give the mayor the benefit of the doubt in the situation, and to an outsider this seems a reasonable point of view.

Knotts' election as mayor came after a campaign in which both parties were divided by bitter factional strife. On the Democratic side this strife was stirred up by a former mayor of Joliet, Illinois, who, it is alleged in some quarters, came to the new steel city for the express purpose of contesting the power of Knotts, and with the encouragement of various steel company officials. Fair-minded men point out, however, that steel company men are to be found in both parties and all factions.

Knotts fairly reflected the general sentiment that the steel company has done much for the city created by its enterprise, but that the people themselves have also done much, and that the city has its own life to live and its own affairs to manage. That there could be any variance of opinion on this score appears curious to the outsider. But a considerable number of people, although not identified with the steel company, have taken the point of view that the company had made the city possible, and therefore ought to have anything it asked for. The company itself disclaims any desire for favors at the hands of the community.

The success in November, 1913, of a fusion ticket " to beat Knotts" was due in large measure, say independent citizens, to the fact that many people who did not believe Knotts to be guilty of bribery and of catering to the saloon, gambling and red-light element, nevertheless had grown tired of the endless strife which centered about him. They felt that it brought odium to the city, and that the city should not continue to suffer merely for the sake of vindicating Knotts. Then, too, many foreign voters were led to support the fusion ticket because they felt that Knotts used high-handed police methods. Even one of Knotts' supporters acknowledges that " a Russianized police force" was a charge that had too much truth in it to be laughed down.

With these two elements added to the opposition which had fought Knotts from the very first, and which included some of the most influential steel company officials, Knotts was at last beaten. That influential men in the steel company and its Gary Land Company really named the fusion ticket and put forth great influence in its behalf is not doubted by fair-minded men on both sides of the struggle. And some emphatically declare that the mill bosses brought pressure on the employees to vote against Knotts. But the success of the effort to beat Knotts does not appear to an outside observer to indicate any lessening of the independent spirit which has characterized the citizenship of Gary in its relation to the industrial control. Dissatisfaction with Knotts among citizens of the independent sort had increased enough to sweep him out of power.

The present mayor is considered by many of these citizens to be " clay in the hands of those about him," and the head of the Gary Land Company is spoken of as the real mayor. This official, who has fought Knotts from the start, has also been president of the Commercial Club since its organization. Many citizens see in this fact and in his methods as president of the club, an effort on the part of the steel company to control the business men of the community. He has helped very effectively, however, in many efforts for civic improvement. And he favored the application of the state housing law to Gary, though his critics might point out that he could have done much to prevent the earlier growth of conditions such as the law now prohibits.

The administration of the present mayor has brought about an improvement in the police and health departments and the abolition of the red-light district which had consisted of about a dozen houses. For a time, however, Gary enjoyed the unsavory distinction of being the only city in the country which permitted the reopening of a vice district after having once abolished segregation. But the citizenship became aroused and this district was again closed — permanently most citizens believe.

The school system of Gary is the city's greatest civic achievement and the special pride of the citizens. Its new methods in school administration have attracted the attention of the entire country and recently led to the selection of the superintendent to suggest improvements in New York City's vocational education and use of school plants.

In the early days of Gary when Broadway was just being laid out and not one permanent house had been erected, Thomas E. Knotts, at that time a member of the town board, was taking a Sunday morning walk along the sand hills flanking the street to be. On meeting a young man and finding him to be a school teacher, he recalled his own school teaching days and thought he would find out what the young man knew about education. "We hadn't talked long," said Knotts, "when I decided to quit and listen." Before they parted the young man was asked whether he would consider a proposition to head the school system of the new city if at some time the offer were made to him.

AN EXAMPLE OF COMMUNITY ACHIEVEMENT AT GARY
The Emerson Public School

The time soon came, and William A. Wirt became superintendent of the Gary schools.

This is not the place to deal with educational theories, or the more technical points or school administration and curricula. But it is worth pointing out that the ·provision for manual training, nature study, playgrounds and leadership, gymnasium equipment, and industrial education of the new town is fully up to the standard set by the most progressive and resourceful cities. The arrangement of school space, study periods, and service of grade and special teachers is devised with rare skill, economy and balance. The space used for some of these modern lines of school work is of the sort which is entirely wasted in many buildings. The time and service of teachers also are so ingeniously planned that no more teachers are required than in many places are employed to handle the same number of pupils merely in the conventional classes. The all-round community value of the future citizen is the goal. With well-timed gradations the play spirit is naturally fused into work impulses.

The public can actually save expense by providing playgrounds, swimming pools, gymnasia, etc., Professor Wirt says, if only their utilization during the school day is well planned. To quote him: " The children that are in the swimming pool at each hour of the day, for instance, would have to have a school-room provided for them if they did not have this swimming pool. Since the swimming pool occupies less valuable space, it costs less than a class-room. It is cheaper, therefore, to the taxpayer to have a swimming pool in the school than not to have one. . . . The playground, gymnasia and manual-training rooms are used every school hour, and all of these cost less per capita than regular class-rooms."

The history of the Gary schools illustrates where

the Steel Corporation fell short in its efforts to anticipate and master the civic needs of the community.
The Jefferson School erected by the company in launch-
ing the town cost $90,000, and as structures go is
doubtless well built.   It was built under pressure, and
the steel company architect was, of course, faced with
an extensive and many-sided problem, on all phases
of which no one man could be a specialist.   But just
as the company brought in no leading expert in city
planning, it failed to gauge the country's advances in
school architecture and call in the best specialist to
be had.   We may have our own surmise, however, as
to the course which would have been pursued if some
particular process in the manufacture of steel had been
in need of equipment.   It is to the credit, therefore,
of the civic intelligence of the town that when the Gary
school board undertook the building of school houses
it retained the architect of the St. Louis schools, generally recognized as one of the foremost men in this
special line in the United States.

He built the Emerson School for the school board,
at a cost of $225,000 for building, site and playground.
This school is declared to be equivalent to five plants
of the Jefferson type.   To serve a population of 100,-
000, which would include approximately 15,000 school
children — and Gary is expected to grow to this extent before many years — eight buildings of the Emerson type would be required, costing for annual maintenance far less than forty buildings of the Jefferson
type.

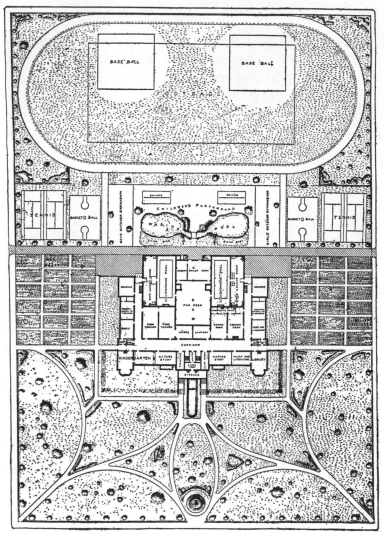

FROEBEL SCHOOL

Located in the midst of Gary's poorest foreign population, this
school serves also as a splendid recreation center.

Gary's finest school, the Froebel, has been built in the midst of the poor foreign population of the south side. It serves both as school and recreation center. The cost was $300,000 and the capacity is 2,700. The spacious ground in front of the building is a public park open at all times. At either side of the building are children's school gardens. A six-acre playground with baseball, basketball and football fields, running track and tennis courts, is in the rear. The auditorium seats 1,000 people. The locker rooms adjoining the swimming pools have a capacity for 1,000 men and 1,000 women in addition to the school boys and girls All the school swimming pools are open two nights a week to women and four nights to men. Auditoriums, playgrounds and swimming pools are open on Sunday afternoons as well as through the week.

The provision of playgrounds, play parks and recreation centers by the schools, leaves the city park commission, created in 1911, free to undertake the work of providing the larger parks. Thus far little has been done. Sometimes spurred on by rumors that the Steel Corporation is to extend its lake front holdings eastward, the citizens rouse themselves periodically to secure some land on the shore of Lake Michigan. Efforts were made by Gary to condemn a tract just east of the present holdings of the company, in the town of Miller, but successful opposition was made by that town. Another project is to make a park along the bed of the Grand Calumet River, south of the city   The plan involves the reclaiming of a couple of thousand acres which are periodically flooded. The digging of the so-called "Burns Ditch" would divert the waters of the river into Lake Michigan several miles east of the city.

The Gary Public Library has from the first rendered most effective civic service both in its first quarters where it occupied a vacant store and conducted English classes for foreigners in the basement, and in its present splendid $65,000 building given by Andrew Carnegie.

A grouping of public buildings has been finely developed on Fifth Avenue. Facing the library is the Y. M. C. A. building, given by Elbert H. Gary. It is the third largest in Indiana and cost $250,000. The equipment and furnishings, which cost $40,000 additional, were a gift from the Steel Corporation. Just east of the Y. M. C. A. is the site of the $125,000 post-office. Though not in this group, another fine building is the steel company hospital, near the mill, which represents the highest type of hospital construction and equipment.

Perhaps the most significant recent development in Gary is the rise of municipal loyalty and coöperation. The growth is more manifest to one who occasionally visits the place than to the inhabitants themselves. The enthusiasm with which citizens of all classes not only serve as committee members or directors of local organizations, but devote time and energy to such activities, shows a marked contrast to the early spirit in which the scramble for individual advantage seemed

Y. M. C. A. Building: Gift of Elbert H. Gary

Public Library: Gift of Andrew Carnegie

uppermost. And it betokens much of civic promise for the future.

It may be that the lack of tradition has made coöperation easy. Few cities could show on a Y. M. C. A. board of trustees a Jew, two Catholics, an Episcopalian and a Presbyterian, all working together harmoniously. And it is not usual to find a Y. M. C. A.

STEEL COMPANY HOSPITAL

secretary serving as manager of a financial campaign which raised in one week more than $40,000 for a Catholic hospital building — the Mercy Hospital — designed to equip the town with facilities for the care of the sick to compare in some degree with the splendid hospital which the company built at the steel mill. The $18,000 for the Presbyterian Neighborhood House, to be sure, was raised almost entirely outside of Gary, but the community evidenced a vigorous interest and hope in what it might soon accomplish. A Slavic-speaking head-resident was placed in charge.

Some effort is being put forth by the other churches also to reach the foreigners of the south side. There is a Polish Catholic church right next to a whole group of shacks. In addition to the denominations mentioned, the Congregational, Baptist, Methodist, Christian, Lutheran, Episcopal and Greek churches are all represented, several having one or more good edifices.

A strong body of citizens has launched an associated charities. Newspapers and commercial organizations are increasingly turning attention to affairs of community betterment.

Gary stands out to-day as the greatest single manifestation of industrial power to be found in America. The Steel Corporation's triumphs in the economics of production are only less impressive than its complete command over the army of workers it employs. These together are exceeded in significance at Gary only by the unparalleled opportunity this vast industrial power possessed to determine the living conditions of a great multitude of human beings.

At Gary, as nowhere else, the opportunity was completely unhampered. The conditions and forces which had to be reckoned with elsewhere did not exist, had not grown up. The hills, which in other places have steadily thwarted expansion, were in Gary only sandy undulations. As if to impress Nature herself that here at least she must be completely subservient, the very landscape was planed level and the watercourses shown their places. Nothing man-made blocked the way. Even the citizens-to-be of the future town were to a large extent within the willing of this industrial power to select. The streets and houses for their habitation, their necessities of life, the conditions under which their children should grow up, and their livelihood might all be determined at the nod of the rulers of steel.

The people of this country are increasingly asking an accounting of the way such power is used. If public welfare asserts its right to keep railroads within bounds in fixing transportation rates, what shall be its attitude toward a power that can fix the whole round of work and home and community conditions for large masses of men, women and children? The industrial executives who created Gary reiterate that their concern was the establishment of a steel mill and allied plants, that into city building they went only so far as necessity compelled. But "only so far" involved the very plan of the city, and many of the fundamentals which would determine its civic growth.

What has been the outcome? It is clear that industrial arrangement had the right of way. In so far as the city interests have not conflicted with industrial plans, or in so far as they were essential to those plans, they have received such attention as the largely self-contained civic enlightenment of steel-makers suggested. If industry needed Lake Michigan frontage, that was sufficient reason to deprive the city of any whatsoever — especially if the impregnability of an industrial fortress was at stake.

The men who are content only with the most scientific, thorough and largest success in shaping steel, thought their own civic rule o' thumb entirely competent to shape the molds for the flow of human life. Their very super-qualities as architects of industry set a standard which the observer craves for and fails to find in the upbuilding of the town. A great industrial power let slip through its giant fingers a chance to work out a civic achievement the like of which the country has not known. The opportunity was exceptional enough to have attracted the thought and service of men whose civic purpose and ability would have commanded the respect and confidence of the nation.

Was paternalism to be avoided? Then a civic construction commission would have been the best and clearest disavowal. Paternalism consists not in the nature and number of things done, but in the spirit and way in which they are done. Gary, the community, could have been better planned, housing could have been more extensively provided, larger civic responsibilities, at less exacting costs of time, could have been shouldered by the industrial leaders through such a planning and construction commission, all with far less paternalism than has been shown in things actually done.

Yet citizenship, at the same time, could have shared civic responsibilities from the outset more largely than was permitted. The creativeness, the appreciation of

human values, which the new townspeople have put
into their schools, are an increment which all the steam
shovels along the lake front could not have dumped
into the melting pot of the growing city.

Nor could they have stirred its idealism as did a
Gary newsboy who risked, and lost, his life that the
skin from his crippled leg might be used in the effort
to save a burned girl.   It is not enough to supply house
paint by the barrel — the poorest little Hungarian
school girl must have opportunity to express the best
she can learn and aspire to.   The tonnage methods of
industry are not adequate for life.

CHAPTER VIII

TOWN BUILDING BY PRIVATE ENTERPRISE

THE recent development of the work suburb stands out strikingly in the fact that an industrial city established as recently as 1871 is yet old enough to have three offshoots which in their respective conditions may be said to typify ancient, medieval and modern history in the rise of the industrial satellite city. For on the outskirts of Birmingham, Alabama, are to be found an old style cotton mill village which barely affords the primitive necessities, a dreary steel town of the eighties, and a type of the best of American industrial suburbs, which applies foresight and modern invention to house and street as well as to shop and sidings, which expresses business genius in the physical basis for community life, even though it lacks the civic statesmanship to conserve to the citizen workers the values created by community growth.

To many Americans the South stands for tradition and for slow change in the established order of things. They think of plantations, of white-columned, gracious houses surrounded by stately trees, of boundless hospitality, of unkempt shanties with swarms of pickaninnies and poor whites, of slow-growing towns and easy-going ways, of occasional cotton mills as the principal manifestation of modern industry. Even if they can picture the "new South" of iron and steel, coal production, and manufactures, they are dominated by older habits of thought. They are quite unprepared to find in the heart of Alabama a "boom" city claiming big factory achievements and commercial progress.

Birmingham reared itself out of the very ground in which it was planted but forty years ago; literally pulled itself up by its own boot-straps — as it hauled iron, limestone, and coal from its own substructure. It was this bold vision which its rugged industrial pioneers caught in the gleam of mineral wealth as their horses' hoofs broke open the surface ore. They had the red dirt examined, coal seams tested, and limestone quarries bared. They saw building stone and clay within easy reach. They heard in imagination the railroads wrestling with their tonnage, and saw a vast people coming to dig and reduce and put into marketable shapes the strength of their hills. And in the valley north of Red Mountain, six years after Appomattox, they laid out in a stubble field a commonplace rectangular street plan for what has now become the South's one big city which knows no heritage of the Civil War. From a population of 3,086 in 1880, the city grew to 38,415 in 1900 and to 132,685 in 1910. Estimates in the year 1914 give it a population of about 175,000.

Birmingham is thus a made-to-order city of our own times; but its makers were mining engineers, prospectors, iron-makers, not millwrights in town building. They laid it out on no different plan from the towns founded fifty years earlier, unwitting of the structural faults those towns had demonstrated and unconscious even that the National Capital, itself a southern city, offered in its diagonal streets, its fine vistas, and time-saving arteries an example of ways to overcome them.

This, of course, is a civic shortcoming not peculiar to Birmingham. Such failure has been the rule rather than the exception in industrial towns in America, even in these days when scores of cities have set out with far-reaching schemes to reshape their structural lines and guide their future growth. This sort of town building in the central city explains in a degree the similar development of two of its satellites, and makes all the more noteworthy the modern methods applied to the third.

Here, then, is the key city of the "new South"— a city built around an industry new to the South in a period that left it no antebellum legacies, a city new at a time when the means for perfecting city building are being most rapidly developed. Her ways of growth and her types of industrial suburbs are bound to mean much not only to her own future but to that of her sister cities.

In the eastern part of Birmingham, closely adjoining the city blast-furnace plant, and the workers' shacks of the Sloss-Sheffield Steel and Iron Company, is the cotton mill village of Avondale, squalid and unkempt. Although now absorbed by the larger city, it still lives in comparative isolation, hiding behind the great mill as if its very shabbiness made it ashamed. The 130 unpainted, down-at-the-heel company houses are homes for the 600 employees of the mill and are owned by B. B. Comer, former governor of Alabama. The rows of box-like houses, mostly one story high, are built on a low flat of cinders. The struggling patches of grass and the lines of small trees in front of the houses only emphasize the barrenness. The mill's smoke and dingy walls seem to oppress the town just as their untoward work conditions overshadow the lives of the workers.

The spaces between the rows of houses, unpaved and without sidewalks, serve as alleys and streets — the alleys distinguished from the streets only by the privies and ash barrels. Wash-tubs, household utensils and babies are around every house. Neither streets nor houses are lighted. No modern system of lighting, water, sewage or sanitation exists. From a few hydrants here and there along the " streets," children wearily lug water pails home. The youngsters fortunately prefer to play around these hydrants, for their other play apparatus at home consists of the family coal pile by the side of the house. A playground was being fitted up in the summer of 1914, but it was doubtful whether equipment would be adequate or play directors would be employed.

A city playground not far away is maintained under two directors, and a public library branch is increasing its influence and usefulness. A small social settlement, Wesley House [1] is doing its best to wrestle with the neighborhood and stimulate such cleanliness as can be secured in the face of heavy odds.

These efforts to improve Avondale are certainly needed. A more depressing neighborhood it would be difficult to find anywhere, or a more forlorn-looking lot of women and children. Some of the people

AT AVONDALE
Two-room box houses for cotton mill workers.

are "poor whites" who wander from mill to mill according as work is full or slack. A considerable number of the women are deserted wives struggling in an

[1] The removal of this agency from another part of Birmingham to Avondale and a larger field of activity, was one of the first tangible results following studies of community and industrial conditions in the Birmingham district, conducted by members of the staff of *The Survey* and published in that magazine for January 6, 1912. "Hell's half-acre," vigorously criticized by *The Survey*, was abolished.

ignorant way to make both ends meet. Many of the households have boarders and ten people in four rooms is not an extreme condition. The older people " dip snuff," and this use of powdered tobacco is frequent among children as well. A tobacco-chewing boy of eight is occasionally found, and a girl of thirteen was with difficulty persuaded to declare that she didn't " aim to do it no more." Some of these habits and ways of living are, of course, brought from the out-of-the-way farms of the hill country, but some are the direct result of the industrialism into which the people come.

Certainly there is little enough in the environment to awaken desire or effort for betterment. But the thing one longs for most as one sees the pallid and dull faces of the children is some rousing " good time " to catch them up in a whirl of real romping fun — to stir their blood into motion, put glow into cheeks and make eyes sparkle. If this is provided by the new play facilities they will be an inestimable boon. But they cannot accomplish all they ought to while Alabama laws permit children to work eleven hours a day.

Ensley, at the other end of Birmingham, is a rectangle of streets flanking the steel mill of the Tennessee Coal, Iron and Railroad Company. Although within the city limits of Birmingham, it is practically a detached community, for there is still much vacant land between it and the built-up part of the city, though the latter is rapidly reaching out. The town, built to accommodate the mill and furnace workers, was laid out in 1886 by a subsidiary of the Tennessee company, the Ensley Land Company — incorporated with power to exercise practically every sort of community function. Until recently, the place, which now has a population of about 18,000, was an industrial barracks like most of the other dreary mill towns of the eighties. But since 1912 there has been a change for the better to which reference will be made.

Contrasting sharply with Avondale and Ensley, dismal civic expressions of the earlier industrialism, is the town of Fairfield. It is doubtful whether there is to be found in America a better planned industrial community. In comparison with its application of modern town planning methods the under-appreciation of the big opportunity at Gary stands out most glaringly.

Fairfield lies just beyond Ensley and has been designed to house the workers in the several new and diversified plants projected by the Tennessee company, the American Steel and Wire Company and other subsidiary companies of the Steel Corporation, con structed to utilize raw materials, pig iron and steel products right on the ground. Here was to be an industrial development eclipsing both Ensley and Bessemer. This scheme, resembling the development at Gary, followed the absorption of the Tennessee Coal, Iron and Railroad Company by the United States Steel Corporation.

After a site for a by-product coke plant had been secured, and additional land for possible expansion had been purchased, the American Steel and Wire Company was assigned to its location. It has completed one of the largest and most modern of wire plants, with safety measures well provided for, up-to-date methods of machinery, and well-equipped offices, café, baths, club-rooms and emergency hospital.

The area secured for the whole development included sufficient land for a town as well as for the whole group of plants. The geographical relation was worked out in such a way as to give the town a site favorable for community development. The observer is not impressed here, as so frequently elsewhere, by the feeling that the factories are given complete precedence, the dwellings being relegated to whatever land happened to be left over. Very evidently the particular site of Fairfield is such that the location of each plant is on land peculiarly suited to it. The wire plant is on a level area on one side of the railroad tracks which connect it with the Ensley mill and a wide shipping region. The town is on a beautifully wooded tract across the railroad — gently rising ground partly overlooking the mill — with the prevailing winds such that they carry mill smoke from the town instead of toward it. It is impossible, of course, to know how far community interests would have counted if industrial advantage had pointed in another direction. But the fact remains, nevertheless, that the arrangement favors home life. The free, wide breathing spaces of Fairfield, the broad avenues of sunlight, far vistas of woods and sky and the grace and charm of clean,

winding, green-bordered streets, and of tree, shrub
and flower grouping — blooming flowers for every
season — all these grant to the little town certain gifts
beyond measure.   Home life has been considered, and
Fairfield makes a radiant contrast to murky Avondale
and Ensley.

The wire plant now employs 1,300 men; the By-
Product Coke Oven plant of the Tennessee company,
600 men; the works of the Harbison-Walker Refractories Company, manufacturing fire brick, 300 men;
and a plant of the Barrett Manufacturing Company,
making by-products from tar received from the coke
ovens, employs 135 men.   It should be noted that,
particularly so far as the wire plant is concerned, there
is little smoke.   The power is largely electricity supplied from the Ensley mill.

In the building of Fairfield the Steel Corporation
did not pursue the policy it had at Gary and elsewhere.
Instead of operating through a subsidiary land company, it put the work in the hands of a local real-
estate firm which organized among Birmingham busi
ness men the Corey Land Company — Corey being the
name originally given to the town.   In this company
the Steel Corporation has no financial interest, nor have
steel officials individually.   The entire responsibility
for the laying-out and development of the town has
thus from the beginning rested on the local real-estate
firm which acted as the operating company for the
Corey Land Company.   This is the Jemison Real Estate and Insurance Company.   Its president, Robert

Jemison, Jr., has taken the keenest interest in making the place a model town.

To this firm the Steel Corporation turned over the land for the town at cost price. Mr. Jemison's first move after visiting other industrial towns in the United States was to secure the services of an expert landscape architect and town planner, George H. Miller, of Boston. The street scheme fitted the topography. Existing tree growth was preserved wherever possible. Different kinds of thoroughfares and secondary streets were designed, each with regard to its specific purpose. Width of pavement was determined by function, with room for expansion. The streets were not curved for the sake of having curved streets but only where it suited the topography or the residents' convenience.

The main entrance thoroughfare is a boulevard 140 feet wide. This leads into the principal business street, 100 feet wide, which connects with a 60-foot county road, a through traffic highway, and emerges from the town at the entrance to the wire plant. Other business and traffic streets are 80 and 50 feet in width. The main residential parkway avenue 100 feet wide, leads through the lowest land to the civic center and thence by a sweeping curve to the upland residential section. Secondary residential streets are 60 and 50 feet wide with narrow roadways and wide planting spaces. Alleys contain the telephone and electric-light poles and the sanitary sewers. The introduction of alleys was opposed by the town planner,

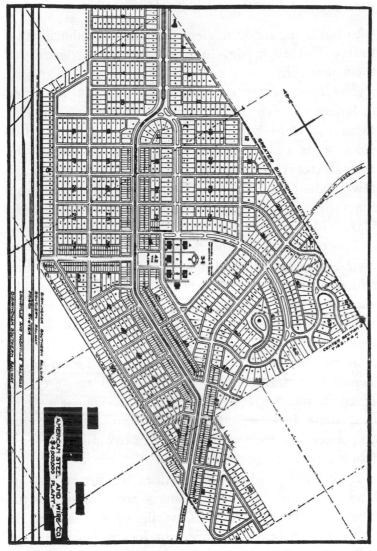

FAIRFIELD'S TOWN PLAN

241

who holds the modern view that they are detrimental to the best town development, but local desire for them prevailed.

The civic center consists of a plaza, a projected grouping of civic buildings and a park. The plaza faces the main business corner and has on its two sides some of the principal business buildings. Its formal tree rows furnish shade and will frame the town hall. The latter will terminate the view from the railroad station up the highway and through the plaza.

The town hall will be the dominant building of the civic group, other buildings for varied municipal and educational purposes forming a quadrangle. The park portion of the civic center has already been provided with recreation facilities, including an athletic field, tennis courts, children's playground with wading pool in a hollow surrounded by trees, and an outdoor gymnasium and running track. Band concerts are given in summer evenings. The schoolhouse will be near these facilities. Other parks are provided, and 90 per cent. of the lots are less than two minutes' walk from a park or parkway area.

A districting scheme determines the use of private lands. Certain kinds of business are confined to the two main business streets, while others dealing in bulky materials are confined to lots adjacent to the railroads and large industries. The residential sections are divided into four main zones with minimum costs of houses stipulated — $1,250, $1,750, $2,500

and $3,000 respectively.   Building lines are prescribed
and many restrictions as to fences, character of buildings, etc.

Before a house was built all the fundamental utilities — streets, sidewalks, water, sewers, gas, electricity, etc.— were installed.   A shrub-planting scheme
extends throughout the entire town.   Flowers, vines
and shrubs in front of cottages built by the real-estate company are designed to harmonize with this
street planting.

All residential lots are fifty feet in width and only
one dwelling house is allowed on each.   These lot
widths and building regulations are very much better
than those in Gary and other industrial towns where
lots twenty-five or thirty feet wide are the rule and
there is no restriction as to the number of buildings on
a lot.

To the eye of the visitor the dwellings in Fairfield
are especially attractive.   The type was set at the beginning by a number of cottages built by the Jemison
company.   It would be hard to find in industrial
America workingmen's dwellings more unlike the
average " company houses."   They range from double
three-room bungalows to two-story residences, all
equipped with bath, hot and cold water, electric light,
and modern sanitary conveniences.   Heating is supplied by furnaces or grates — which in many cases are
sufficient because of the mild climate.   The three-
room bungalows rent for $12 a month, detached four-
room bungalows for $16, five-room for $20, six-room

for $25, and seven- and eight-room two-story dwellings for $35 and $40.

About three hundred houses have already been built on Fairfield's 1,256 lots. They include some erected by the Jemison Company, a number by Birmingham investors, seventy-five for American Steel and Wire Company employees and thirty-one for Tennessee Coal, Iron and Railroad Company employees. Such real estate as is owned by any interest of the Steel Corporation is in the hands of the Tennessee Land Company, a subsidiary of the Tennessee Coal, Iron and Railroad Company. It purchases lots, builds houses, and rents or sells to employees. While effort is made to sell homes on installments to the workingmen who are coming to Fairfield, the contract for the sale of lots by the real-estate company includes no such safeguards as are to be found, for example, in the contracts of the Gary Land Company. The houses sold by the Tennessee Land Company, however, are covered by such safeguards. Should the purchaser be discharged or voluntarily leave the employ of the Steel Corporation, he can receive all the money he has paid for the house, with interest at six per cent., less a reasonable deduction for rental.

The size of the lots and the provision that there shall be but one house on a lot insure plenty of space around each dwelling. Front yards are planned with special reference to the street scheme. But even more thought has been put into the back yards. These are laid out carefully so as to provide vegetable gardens,

HOUSING FOR STEEL WORKERS AT FAIRFIELD
Five-room bungalows for skilled steel workers rent at $19.50 to
$25.00 a month.

THE PLAZA AT FAIRFIELD

laundry yards, flower walks and playground areas for small children — pleasant substitutes for ashes, tin cans and rubbish.

It is significant that the landscape architect for the Jemison Company has considered this back-yard planning as worthy of no less skill than the town framework. He has repeatedly urged its importance and called attention particularly to the possibilities of the vegetable gardens. He states that through such a system developed by one near-by industrial concern, no less than $30,000 worth of vegetables were raised in one year, and he estimates that if vegetable gardens were developed on three quarters of the back yards in Fairfield, as they have been on some, produce could be raised each year to the value of $76,000. Employees living in houses owned by the Tennessee Coal, Iron and Railroad Company in the various mining camps have 1,200 gardens, stimulated first by the building of wire fences around the yards and by cash prizes. These prizes are no longer offered, but in lieu thereof gardens are plowed free for those who care to plant them.

Mr. Miller's emphasis on arrangement of yard space naturally leads to inquiry as to why dwellings have not been grouped so as to make possible a pooling of some of the back-yard space for communal use of the families for playground and other purposes. Plans of this sort were considered, but dangers and delays were foreseen in developing such communal use of land, and the plans were not adopted. While those familiar with the success of the English garden suburb developments along this line might wish that this planning had been given a trial at Fairfield, it is of course true that the advantages to be gained are more needed in the case of houses on smaller lots.

Since Fairfield has been settled there has been gratifying coöperation among the residents in maintaining the attractiveness so intelligently and enthusiastically provided. A civic improvement league was soon organized, and a number of block societies having the same purpose began to care for gardens, lawns, trees and shrubs. A community spirit is rapidly developing.

But the influence of this first well-planned industrial town in the South is not merely local. It is seen in better planned homes and residential subdivisions of Birmingham, in the improvement of the mines, towns, villages and camps, all through the Birmingham district — notably the mining towns Edgewater, Docena, Fossil, Muscoda and Bayview (in construction) belonging to the Tennessee company, which in systems of sanitation, livable conditions and attractive surroundings strike the high mark of modern mine camp development; in the town of Kaulton — built near Tuscaloosa by the Kaul Lumber Company; in the projected plans for Acipco and Tarrant City, industrial communities surrounding the plants of the American Cast Iron Pipe Company and the United States Cast Iron Pipe Company; and above all in the efforts to make Ensley more livable.

Ensley, near enough to watch Fairfield develop before its eyes, roused itself from its dreariness and did more in two years than in the preceding twenty to better its conditions. There has been a veritable epidemic of cleaning up, grass and tree planting, painting and repairing, and sanitary improvements. Vacant lots have been plowed and planted so that in place of mud holes and rubbish heaps are now to be found little fields of oats, corn, cotton or peas. Some of this has no doubt been due to prizes offered in 1910 and 1911 by the Tennessee company for the most attractive yards in Ensley. The old Ensley hotel, an eyesore, was torn down and a group of stores of modern design put in its place. The Ensley park has blossomed out anew and a playground has been established with a play-leader in charge. Two other well-equipped playgrounds — one for white and one for colored children — are provided near the Tennessee company's steel plant. These playgrounds, however, have been without directors. Many gracefully designed bungalows have been built, so that parts of Ensley now look almost as if they belonged to Fairfield. The old hospital has been regenerated inside and out. It was taken from the hands of a contract doctor and now is leased and operated by the Tennessee company. A new high school, the Wesley House social settlement — similar to the one at Avondale — and the Ensley Barraca Association are all new agencies for social and educational betterment which did not exist in 1911. Coal and iron men, steel company

officials, business men and home-owners all coöperated
to rid the town as far as possible of its dismal appearance and develop cleaner, more sanitary and more
attractive conditions.

But with all its admirable town planning and provision for home life Fairfield has some serious shortcomings.   It fails to provide low-priced housing for
low-paid unskilled labor.   It has not safeguarded its
dwellers from real-estate speculation.   And it has
failed to preserve for the people some of the community values, in land and franchises, created by themselves.   These are shortcomings, however, to be found
in practically all of our industrial towns and our general community development as well.

Steel Corporation officials frankly admit that they
have not solved the problem of low-priced housing for
low-paid unskilled men.   While the proportion of such
employees is not large, nothing has been done so far at
Fairfield to make provision for them.   They live here
and there throughout the Birmingham district —
wherever they can get quarters within their means.
Yet the reason given by the Steel Corporation for its
failure to provide for them — that they are foreigners
unaccustomed to American standards of living, that
they have low wages, and that they hoard money for
the use of their families or themselves in their native
lands, and so live on a plane below that which their
employers aim to bring within their reach — are the
very reasons why they should be provided with good
housing and educated as to its value and how to use it.

While it is doubtlessly true that their living conditions are no worse than those of other similarly paid workingmen in Birmingham, the fact remains that the very men most in need of help in securing good housing accommodations are the ones to whom the least help has been given. And with incomes least able to bear the additional charge of carfare, they are forced by the establishment of the better houses for skilled men near the plant to find their habitation farthest from their work.

Several groups of block houses in the lowest priced building zone of Fairfield were originally planned to accommodate the unskilled workers of the American Steel and Wire Company plant, the houses to be built by this company. Much study was put upon the designs to secure a result in keeping with the attractive homes occupied by the skilled men and their families. The buildings, two stories high with roof gardens, were to be fireproof and arranged around court-yards. Rents were not to exceed two dollars a month for each room. But on the eve of construction the plan was halted — as were the other additional housing projects in the hands of the Tennessee Land Company, pending the outcome of the government suit to dissolve the Steel Corporation. The entire progress of Fairfield has been retarded by this circumstance and by the general untoward fortunes of the community at large. The town has simply been marking time, in a sense, and this is expected to continue until the outcome of the suit is determined.

The failure to provide for the housing needs of the unskilled also concerns the negroes, who supply a considerable proportion of such labor.   Fairfield itself is shut against negroes; the very first restriction applying to every lot reads that " said lot shall be used by white persons only, except that any servants employed on the premises may occupy servants' houses."   But just over the city line from Fairfield are clusters of negro shanties which make an unkempt and squalid contrast with the town itself.

Speculative real-estate profits may often indicate the extent to which the interests of the worker are subordinate to business enterprise.   In Fairfield as in many another industrial town the needs of the coming population were shrewdly advertised to money-making middlemen.   Lots were sold to Birmingham investors on the basis that they could be resold at a handsome profit to the workers from Cleveland, Pittsburgh and other steel regions who would be brought down to operate the new plant.

The real-estate company should not necessarily be blamed for this levying of profits for the future home-owner to pay.   True, it received land at cost price from the Steel Corporation and was charged with the responsibility of creating a town for the steel workers. But whatever profits it could make in so doing would certainly be considered as legitimate business and as in accord with the purpose of a real-estate company to earn as much for its stockholders as possible.   The heavy investment in town planning and the installation of fundamental utilities before a single inhabitant was on the ground may have necessitated some quick return, through the sale of lots, in order to carry out the undertaking. And the further point might be made that the activity of these individual investors was necessary if houses in sufficient number were to be ready when the population came. As a matter of fact, the unforeseen delays which arose before the plant of the steel and wire company was completed and put into operation caused the large investment in the town to remain idle for many months, involving a heavy burden for the real-estate company to carry.

From the standpoint of the common welfare the question does not concern the real-estate company's methods so much as the lack of that civic statesmanship which in Europe is beginning to regard housing not as an affair of real-estate speculation but as a community necessity financed with capital at a low rate and developed in the interest of the people who are in need of homes.

The sale of Fairfield lots to speculative investors may have been advantageous or necessary from the standpoint of real-estate enterprise. But what it meant for the coming home-dwellers the advertisements of the real-estate company itself make clear. When the town was beginning to take shape, but long before any of the permanent population of working-men had arrived, the advantages of investment in Fairfield lots were attractively set forth to Birmingham investors. The hundreds of workers soon to come would need homes. Investors "who purchase now and build will reap a handsome return on the investment. The rents alone will pay remarkably good interest, and the property itself should more than double in value shortly."

Accordingly in June, 1910, some three hundred lots were sold. "Many shrewd real-estate investors in Birmingham and elsewhere were numbered among the first purchasers." A list of some of them, including well-known local capitalists, was published. A few months later it was announced that "hundreds of people made real-estate investments with which they are thoroughly satisfied, and those who bought with a view to selling for a profit have been enabled to do so in many instances, for a number of lots have changed hands at a profit of from 25 to 100 per cent." Again it was pointed out that the property would "advance in value greatly." For "the completion of the American Steel and Wire Company plant will give permanent employment to about 1,500 men, the great majority of whom are skilled laborers drawing good wages." These would all need houses in Fairfield, as would also many employees of the Harbison-Walker Refractories Company and the hundreds of men to be employed by the by-product coke ovens nearing completion.

"Fortunes have been made in Birmingham and Ensley real estate," reads another statement addressed to investors. "What happened at Ensley and in Birmingham will be repeated at Corey (Fairfield). More than one man who bought lots at Corey a year ago has realized 100 per cent. on his investment already. Others have sold their lots for profits of from 50 to 90 per cent., and there has been a ready sale for all lots that the owners would sell." And many such instances have been given as the following, published in July, 1914: " Recently a profit of $1,500 was made on a Fairfield lot that has been held less than five months. This property was bought by . . . for $3,-500 and was sold to . . . for $5,000. His investment earned him $300 per month for the time he held it, which is more than 6 per cent. on $5,000 invested for twelve months."

No comment is needed to show what this rise of real-estate values, created by the fact that a working population was coming, meant in rents and home costs for that population to pay. This contrasts most vividly with the consideration shown to the industries in shielding them from high costs. The old city boundaries of Birmingham had significant jogs, leaving two furnaces outside and thus exempt from city taxation. And even the present city line leaves its logical direction so as to exempt the big Ensley furnace plant and steel mill. It was felt that the Tennessee company deserved this special privilege because it was modernizing its plant at large cost and must compete with the well-equipped mills of the North. Similarly the wire plant and other developments of the Steel Corporation at Fairfield are outside the Birmingham boundaries.

In other words, a few large corporations, but not all, are exempted from the penalty which a general property tax, here as in most American cities, places upon the men who build factories or houses or other improvements. Efforts to overcome this disability in attracting capital for industrial investment are natural, but such a system of gerrymandering in favor of the big industries puts a double damper upon small and diversified industries which might be located within the city borders and would have to pay city taxes. Until Birmingham succeeds in removing such a taxation penalty from all improved real estate, transferring it to land held for speculation and imposing it on real estate which derives its excess value from the sheer fact of city growth — as Vancouver is doing, in line with a settled policy that has been adopted throughout Europe — the unfairness of letting the rest of the community carry the load which the few escape by boundary jogs is all too plain.

The granting of a perpetual street-railway franchise on the principal street of Fairfield before the town was born was still less defensible than the effort for speculative profits in real estate. Here again was value based solely on the needs of the coming people. Ordinary justice should have left for them the right to dispose of value created by themselves. The fact that the Birmingham Railway, Light and Power Company had a perpetual franchise in Birmingham was no excuse in these days when the struggle of a score of cities to preserve their rights to their streets has led to a country-wide acceptance of the principles of short-term franchises, adequate compensation to the city in direct revenue or lower fares, and reservation by the city of power to regulate service.

If the uncertainties of the future seemed to afford any warrant in the early days of Birmingham for perpetual franchises the same plea cannot be urged for Fairfield. Development there was assured by the plans and investment of the Steel Corporation. Yet on the pretext that broad terms must be given to induce the Birmingham company to "pioneer" at Fairfield, a perpetual franchise was given by the county authorities after a contract on that basis had been made between the company and the real-estate company. Fairfield at that time was still unincorporated and thus not affected by the thirty-year limitation which the state of Alabama has imposed on franchises granted in cities. The fact that several men are interested in both railway and real-estate companies is frankly given in explanation of the matter-of-course way in which the interests of the future community were ignored in the contract between the two companies. And the county authorities seem to have made no effort to obtain good terms for the public.

It is pointed out that the Birmingham company has not been given exclusive rights in Fairfield, since another company has been granted a franchise on other streets. But the Birmingham company's franchise is exclusive so far as the main street is concerned. And furthermore it has been given perpetual though not exclusive franchise rights covering the supply of gas and electric current.

Subordination of community welfare to business interest at Fairfield, as manifest in the speculative real-estate profits and the granting of the street-railway franchise in perpetuity, points insistently to the need for alert public authority and new civic statesmanship in guiding community growth. Yet the desirability of such larger public concern should rest not so much upon the need for protection against business exploitation as upon the value of assuring more general application of the modern town planning which is so well exemplified at Fairfield. Adequate safeguarding of public interests is an important and clearly recognized function of government, but we are only beginning to understand how much can be achieved if the governmental agency is used not merely to safeguard but to promote public welfare. Forethought and skill were used by an up-to-date and enthusiastic real-estate company in building Fairfield according to the best plans it could devise. Why should not the same intelligence be applied to all the growth of Birmingham and her industrial satellites — as could be done through the adaptation of the principles of the British Town Planning Act and the services of expert town planners which such a measure would put at the disposal of the public?

In contrasting the development in Birmingham and Fairfield with the newer English housing schemes and methods of town building and extension, it would be unfair not to take account of the fundamentally different conditions. Birmingham, Alabama, is a newly developed part of a young country, where capital commands high interest rates, 6 to 8 per cent. being normal, and where the supply of capital for proper development is inadequate. England, on the other hand, is an old country with capital so abundant that it is content with interest rates half as high, and even so must seek foreign investment in order to be fully employed. Birmingham is typical of America with its fresh start and on-rushing progress. Slower-moving England, building upon the foundations of centuries, has latent resources of time and money and interest to work out the new methods of town planning. In Birmingham quick results seemed all important.

The real-estate company at Fairfield has shown, as we have seen, intelligence and skill and appreciation of human needs, much above the average in real-estate operations. And this involved difficult problems. For the better way had to be explained convincingly to such stockholders as may have thought the old real-estate profit-making methods adequate. Views not only of stockholders and directors but of city and county officials, of utility corporations, and of wage-earners of various wage-earning capacities, all had to be met. To "get results" satisfactory to all and carry out their own conception of the best plans was the problem of the executives, and naturally it involved modifications. As the saying goes, " It is hard to get all the squirrels up one tree."

Yet the very fact that, owing to industrial hazards, the real-estate company has yet to pay a dividend, brings out the fundamental point quite as clearly as if speculative profits boasted on certain lots had been made on the whole property. That fundamental point is the need for considering the development of our new industrial towns not from the standpoint of real-estate enterprise with risk of loss or possibility of large profit, but from the standpoint of statesman-like provision for human need. Houses for people are just as essential as any of the things a city must have, and the provision of them ought to be as sure an undertaking — and involving as much public concern — as any that might warrant municipal bonds. If left to private enterprise the investment ought to be on a similarly solid basis, for housing is not a commodity which people may do without or not as they please, but is just as necessary as the provision of water or transportation or any other fundamental utility. Governmental loaning arrangements similar to those in Great Britain, and standards such as are provided by the British Town Planning Act would start America on the same road as that which England is traveling — of statesmanship in town planning.

Birmingham was named for the city which prides itself on being the workshop center of England. Both Birminghams are in important coal regions of their respective countries; and both are manufacturing points for steel products. The similarities of location and purpose which led Alabama industrial pioneers to name their new city after its English prototype have been followed by striking civic similarities and contrasts. By a coincidence, the very year in which the Alabama Birmingham extended its boundaries and adopted the commission form of government, was the same year in which the British Birmingham increased its own area, taking in six outlying communities, and simplified its government through merging eighteen poor relief authorities into two and consolidating six local councils, three county councils, five tramway authorities, three electricity authorities, five burial boards, several joint sewage commissions and six town planning authorities into one unified town council.

But this English municipality affords a most striking contrast to the Alabama Birmingham, and indeed to every other American city, in its comprehensive and constructive housing policy. Three garden suburbs typify the new standard in city homes — Bourneville, the model industrial town built by Cadbury, the cocoa manufacturer; Harborne, an excellent example of the co-partnership principle; and Bordsley, one of the best English housing developments not involving co-partnership but adhering to individual home ownership. But even more significant is the application of modern town planning methods to all the city's growth, through the provisions of the British Town Planning Act. Birmingham has planned the development of much of her suburban area. Not only are street systems and public open spaces established to meet the needs of the community as a whole, but the number of houses per

acre is definitely limited.   Birmingham has thus taken
greater advantage of the act than any other city.

In the congested city center a municipal housing department is achieving notable results in slum regenera-
tion.   In seven years it demolished 1,457 houses as
unfit for human habitation, caused 1,846 to be repaired,
and removed 258 so as to give light and air around
neighboring dwellings.   Birmingham, Alabama, has
the opportunity to deal with the wooden beginnings of
such a situation before it is intrenched in the brick
and mortar which the English Birmingham had to hew
asunder or chisel into shape.

Here, then, is an English municipality's well-bal-
anced program for better housing — the pioneering
experiments in town building, the application of tested
methods to all the city's growth, and the reconstruc-
tion of those parts of the city center which most need
improvement.

This comprehensive housing policy of Birmingham
is due in large measure to the vision and initiative of
John S. Nettlefold.   Through investment of his
means, his time and his imagination he demonstrated
to his townsmen the practicability of town planning.
He started Harborne on co-partnership tenants' association lines.   Critics gave it just three years to get
into the bankruptcy court.   He took just that time to
make the undertaking an assured financial success.
As member of the town council his administrative skill
devised the methods which have made the municipal
housing department so effective in dealing with the

bad housing of the city center, and the same genius he devoted to the work of applying the national town planning act to the outskirts of the city. His books on " Practical Housing " and " Practical Town Planning " have extended the large influence he has had in the British movements these books serve.

Suggestive for America is the example of this civic statesman and the city he has made so noteworthy a leader in housing and town planning effort. The planning of our industrial towns and their community scheme of organization should command the ablest coöperative effort of public-spirited citizens, industrial leaders and public authorities. No problem more concerns the daily well-being of the mass of the people.

CHAPTER IX

COMMUNITY PLANNING

THESE sketches of industrial towns on the rims of cities have brought us to a point where we see clearly that the suburb which the city dweller hits off as a " satellite " is more than a sporadic fragment of civic cosmos. It is one manifestation, and the most easily seen, of the great concentric outer rings of industry which powerful economic forces are flinging out from the congested centers.

It has been possible to give close examination to only a few " satellite cities." Those selected have been of varied types — Pullman, as the most striking early example of the half-isolated paternalistic town, which has been overtaken and submerged by larger urban growth as well as by the democratic forces innate in municipal life; certain Cincinnati suburbs, where manufacturing plants have gained the advantages of the " open," while workers have largely been left behind in the big city's tenements; St. Louis' " east side," favored by special factors which make for economic gain while other factors spell civic isolation; Gary, greatest instance of a made-to-order community, with an unhampered opportunity at the disposal of its creators; and Fairfield, with its modern town planning but lack of that civic statesmanship which assures to the whole community the values created by its own growth and which develops the intelligent exercise of public authority in guiding urban extension.

The rapidity of all this extraordinary development stands out. While the material for these sketches was being collected, plans matured for a great industrial district across the river to the north of Kansas City, 3,500 acres in area. In a few months 2,509 acres were allotted for factory sites. The Western Electric Company moved its New York manufacturing department to the big plant on the outskirts of Chicago, thus concentrating all manufacturing in the huge shops at Hawthorne. So, too, the Crane Company developed plans to concentrate its Chicago plants on the city's southwestern outskirts.

This rapidity partly explains why the movement goes ahead all but unnoticed by social workers, revolutionary though it is. The head of a social settlement in the Middle West writes:

I was surprised when I realized that I could not give you the slightest accurate information without a visit to some of our near-by towns. I have talked with some of our workers, but this problem seems to be an entirely new thought to all of them as it was to me. We see facts which are worthy of study here and which make us realize that we have never given consideration to this aspect of our city growth.

His reply is typical of others received in answer to inquiries addressed to civic leaders. It has prompted further explorations which have revealed situations resembling those to which these articles have directed attention.

From Harrisburg we learn that the " execrable housing conditions " of the lower reaches of the capital city of Pennsylvania are being reproduced in the newer and adjacent Steelton which employs from 8,000 to 15,000 men. A social worker's observations beyond Cleveland's city boundaries show a town with meager planning and social equipment; some of the employees in the two industries living in monotonously similar company houses and some of them making the short trip out from Cleveland each day.

The region around Pittsburgh contains fifty towns which serve as examples of the absence of town planning. Vandergrift, forty miles away, shows well-designed provision for the skilled, clerical and professional workers, the company getting all the increment of land values, while the unskilled are left to shift in an unplanned neighboring community. Two recent developments are Midland, where the Crucible Steel Company is laying out a model addition; and Aliquippa, where the Jones and Laughlin Company is building a brand-new town. On the heels of the report of a new steel mill and town to be built near Duluth came the news of another big plant to be located in Canada just across the river from Detroit.

From Seattle comes the information that newly arising industries are locating at the city's edge or beyond. A typical outlying settlement is Edmunds, eight miles out, which boasts at once of its nearness to Seattle and of its advantage in being outside the area of congestion. Already it has many woodworking factories and a steel and bolt plant, and seems destined to be a city of manufactures and working people. Its slogans are: " No saloons and an empty jail." " A chorus of factory whistles is the city's rising call."

To offer new industries the advantage of the city, with the low costs of outlying sites, the Seattle Chamber of Commerce entered into an arrangement with the county officials whereby factory locations at moderate rental might be obtained on what was once the county farm.

Just outside the city limits of Portland, Oregon, a beef packing plant was built a few years ago. A connection was made with the street railway of Portland and a town has grown up. It had little planning beyond that which the average real-estate dealer uses in plotting out lots. This opportunity for guiding city growth seems to have been missed by the Portland business men who have recently had a comprehensive city plan prepared for the widening of several Portland streets and the development of an extensive park system.

Rapid and far-flung, the movement of industry to city outskirts reaches deep into the common life — deeper than is as yet recognized. It has potencies for good and evil, lends itself as readily as a land boom to glowing images, and as readily dwindles off into cold fact. On one hand we have the point of view which, with keen perception of the new methods of town planning, President Johnson of the Baldwin Locomotive Works displayed in a recent address to the people of Chester; on the other we find the plight in which the working people of a Standard Oil town found themselves recently in Missouri. Mr. Johnson explained in detail the locomotive company's plan of development at Eddystone, which adjoins Chester and forms practically a part of it, where several departments of the works have been located. He said that the development at Eddystone had been quite as rapid as the supply of labor at Chester justified. He continued:

Of 6,840 men employed at Eddystone, it was ascertained that 3,555 were residents of Chester, 505 were residents of suburban districts between Chester and Philadlephia, and 2,780 were residents of Philadelphia, finding transportation to Eddystone over the Pennsylvania, the Philadelphia and Reading, and the trolley lines.

The question is how to induce these 2,780 men, who are content to reside in Philadelphia, and travel back and forth daily, to move their homes to Chester and become a part with you in developing your city. To do this you must make your city attractive as a place of residence. You must curb the traffic in intoxicating drinks . . . you must cultivate a spirit of obedience to the laws, which would make impossible the conditions which brought the name of Chester unfavorably before the entire community during your trolley strike. You must elect to your public offices, men of the highest type, who will place the public interest before any private interest. You must make your city beautiful and attractive; you cannot leave this to the unrestricted enterprise of the individual. You must join in the awakening which is taking place all over America for improvements in town planning, in housing, in schools, parks and other things contributing to the public welfare. . . .

I would like to see a carefully considered plan of development for both the cities of Philadelphia and Chester; and for the entire district between them, defining their street planning, roads, parks and docks so that it may all be developed as one whole, rather than as a group of independent, segregated boroughs.

The other side of the picture shows the risk and uncertainty which a workman assumes in taking a homeowner's stake in an industrial community. The insecurity of community life based on the prosperity of one concern or even of one industry stands out when towns are stranded through accident, as in the case of Cherry, Illinois, or through the decline of an industry, as in the case of some Michigan lumber towns, or through the abandonment of a plant.

Not long ago a Missouri court room heard a plea for the life of the Standard Oil Company in that state, made on behalf of the work-people of Sugar Creek, its made-to-order town on the bank of the Missouri River. The existence of the town was threatened by the campaign to " oust the monopoly " from Missouri. It was stated in the court that " most of the employees built cottages for themselves ranging in value between $500 and $3,500." " The wealthy Standard Oil Company," said one inhabitant, " will not feel the court's decision nearly as much as we, who built our little homes here and are trying to rear our children properly. If the plant closes, property in this town will not be worth ten cents on the dollar." " It isn't easy," said another, " to sit still and see the savings of years swept away." A third inhabitant added:

And now the insurance companies are talking of taking away our insurance. They are afraid some workman who is going to lose his place will set it afire to get the insurance and the town might burn. The Standard Oil Company has been good to us; it paid for the piano in the school house and furnished the school with fuel the first year after it was built. It pays $200 a year toward the salary of the Methodist preacher and gave a stove and the fuel to the church. For seven years the company has kept a large hack with two horses, and twice a week it sends it to Independence with all the women who want to go shopping there and it hauls them back.

Since the decision of the courts in favor of the company, the latter has materially increased its development at Sugar Creek.

The problem, then, is one not merely of scientific physical planning but also of civic independence. And it involves the whole social scheme of an industrial people. For the most part, as our study of these expanding industrial areas has shown, we have left this intricate problem to real-estate speculators and the industrial captains, who frankly say that their interest in the civic side of their concerns is incidental. The result produced by these forces has usually proved inadequate and socially unintelligent.

The methods of real-estate speculation, with immediate profits as the main object, are analogous to the wastefulness with which our forests in pioneer days were despoiled. At its worst this exploitation gives us the hideous shacks at Gary, with their profits of 50 per cent. squeezed out of immigrants packed two and three and even more to the room. Little better are the " builders' rows " of flimsy frame boxes, which every industrial suburb and the outskirts of every large city can show. Even at their best, the ordinary real-estate methods either fail to serve the workers because larger profits may be made in supplying homes to other classes, or else heap middlemen's profits on the home buyer who can least afford to pay them.

In a Cincinnati suburb we have seen vacant land around factories which had moved out from the city's center, used not for homes for the workers in these factories but for the dwellings of people whose work is in the heart of the city. At Fairfield, with all its excellent town planning, the company which developed the place for the Steel Corporation urged upon Birmingham investors the advantage of buying property in the town which could be sold at a good profit when the workingman should come to live in it.

This same levying of profits for the workingman to pay is seen in connection with a new suburb of Los Angeles. Finely laid out on a 3,000-acre tract, with advice from a city planner of national prominence, it is designed to provide for a large expected manufacturing development. Circulars to Los Angeles investors describe it as " the city with the payroll," and they are informed of the " profits to be derived from an investment in that growing city." For " during the present year industries have been secured, assuring a working force of three thousand men and a population conservatively placed at 10,000 within a few years, and it is fair to assume that factories providing employment for an equal number of skilled mechanics and laborers will be secured for 1913 and 1914."

The factory gains by this transfer to the city's edge. We know that because the outward movement gathers force. The city gains in the relief the movement brings to its arteries of trade; industrial freight does not have to be choked through its central valves. The social problem then is whether community interests receive attention commensurate with the foresight, skill and ingenuity devoted to securing the utmost industrial advantage; whether the shift for the thousands of working people away from the city pressure is to bring an increment of better living, easier living — a lifting of the standards of industrial civilization; or whether, for the great mass, it is merely another swapping of the frying pan for the fire.

The material collected for these studies is not enough to warrant an attempt to answer the searching questions put in the first chapter. If this setting forth of the situation has led to a sharper and clearer definition of the problems involved, it will have served its purpose. These problems can be recapitulated briefly. They relate to:

1. Public control over the industrial frontiers of a modern city.

2. City planning as it applies to these suburban divisions individually and as part of the greater city.

3. Taxation and the private exploitation of mounting land values.

4. Demand for capital for home building at low rates of interest.

5. Home ownership and the workers' mobility.

6. Recreational and social requirements of the outlying communities.

7. Unemployment as affected by isolated industries.

8. Perplexing questions of social self-dependence and industrial autocracy.

9. The relation between the satellite and the common civic and community purpose of the industrial district.

While in the large these problems are all but neglected, the investigations on which these chapters are based reveal large constructive forces at work. Not the least of these are the industrial forces themselves.

Enterprises like the " factory colony " on the outskirts of Cincinnati, the Clearing-Argo factory district on the outskirts of Chicago and the ingenious Bush Terminal plant in New York which gives small manufacturers the advantage of wholesale provision of space, power and shipping facilities, illustrate the imagination and genius of those manufacturers and engineers who planned an escape from city congestion and gained efficient and economical factory conditions outside the great city; and enterprises like these cannot fail to afford many favorable social advantages.

Similarly, there are signs of enlarging vision and social appreciation in the other great economic interests. The haphazard and socially unintelligent methods of many real-estate operators have been vigorously discussed by a real-estate operator himself.

In an address [1] before the National Association of Real Estate Exchanges, J. C. Nichols of Kansas City said:

The subdividing of land for city purposes in practically all American cities is generally left to chance and private and selfish interests. City authorities have to some extent made certain general requirements as to a reasonable continuity and regularity of streets; but little has been done toward a good, wholesome, general city plan of.subdivision.

The best manner of subdividing land should not necessarily mean the quickest sale. The destiny and growth of your town is largely affected by the foresight of the man who subdivides the land upon which you live.

It is easy enough to name your addition, file your plat, take your lots and advertise them for sale to those who may wish to buy; but it is a more difficult matter to decide just what should be within that property, not only to-day but twenty-five years from to-day — the class of houses, their architectural design, distance from the

---

[1] This address has been published in pamphlet form by the American Civic Association, Washington, D. C.

street, what character of outbuildings, location of telephone poles, location of churches and schools, provision
of playgrounds, open centers for flowers and shrubbery,
concealing of the street-car lines in parkways, and erec-
tion of suitable shelters along the line, the decoration of
the streets with ornamental lights, placing of neighborhood stores in unobjectionable points, selection of the best
type of street improvements for residence streets, and
the creation of civic and local improvement associations
that will be sufficiently alert to protect every restriction
and keep alive the interest and enthusiasm that exists in
the addition when new.

Referring to his own development of a thousand-
acre residential tract in Kansas City, Mr. Nichols explained the many restrictions stipulated in the arrangement of houses and use of lots.   These are welcomed
by individual purchasers as a protection to their best
interests rather than an invasion of their rights.   " In
the early days," said Mr. Nichols, " I was afraid to
suggest restrictions; now I cannot sell a lot without
them."

The emphasis which American town planners are
beginning to put on definite schemes for the development of outlying neighborhoods — for constructive
city building — is especially encouraging.   They have
heretofore concerned themselves chiefly with elaborate
schemes for reconstructing the congested centers of
our cities, widening streets and cutting new avenues,
providing extensive boulevard and park systems, and
capturing our imaginations with magnificent groupings

of public buildings. Such plans are now being supplemented with the even more necessary efforts to guide the natural expansion of the cities.

A competition recently held by the City Club of Chicago and a study conducted by a special committee of the National Conference on City Planning have given stimulus to this tendency. The conditions in the Chicago competition confined it clearly to the problem of developing unimproved residential property for people of small or moderate means on the outskirts of the city. Each competing city planner was " given " a quarter-section — one hundred and sixty acres — on level, treeless prairie, with street cars on two sides making the eight-mile trip " downtown " in forty-five minutes; surrounding ·property subdivided in the prevailing gridiron fashion; scattered groups of frame and brick houses within a mile; large industrial plants half a mile to four miles distant, many of them within twenty minutes by foot or street car. Each plan was to show street arrangement and width, grass plots, fore gardens or planting of trees along them; size and arrangement of lots; location of dwellings; gardens; open spaces other than streets; and spaces for business, recreational, educational, religious, administrative and other social needs.

The hope was expressly stated that some of the plans might be adopted as the basis for actual developments. Thirty-nine plans were submitted from competitors in fourteen different cities. The first prize was won by Wilhelm Bernhard of Chicago; the second

prize by Arthur C. Comey of Cambridge, Massachusetts, and the third prize by Mrs. Ingrid Lilienberg and
Albert Lilienberg, chief of the town planning department, Gottenberg, Sweden. An especially hopeful
result of the competition is the fact that the City Club
of Chicago has received many inquiries from manufacturers in various parts of the country desirous of
getting information on practical plans for housing
workmen in sanitary, attractive and inexpensive cottages.

The study conducted by the National Conference
on City Planning represents a year's work by a committee which submitted with its report nine plans
from nine groups of participants in the study. The
conditions laid down for this study were similar to
those of the Chicago City Club competition as regards
the character of the site and the broad lines of development, but they went much further in specifying
the cost of the land at $2,500 an acre, the cost of such
fundamental utilities as sewers, the provision of lighting and other public-service facilities, and the rent
to be expected from the prospective inhabitants.
" The majority of the families will occupy dwellings
commercially rentable at from $15 to $30 a month,
while there must be provision for some families who
cannot afford to pay $15, and for a considerable mi-
nority who will demand residences rentable at from $30
to $100 a month or occasionally even higher." It
was stipulated that developments were to be governed
by the requirements defined in the building code ap-

CITY OUTSKIRTS — HAPHAZARD OR PLANNED?

A committee of the National Conference on City Planning
enlisted nine groups of participants in a year's study. This shows
one of the nine suggested plans for an outlying area.

277

proved by the National Board of Fire Underwriters and also in the model housing law as proposed by the National Housing Association. The plans were accompanied by detailed figures covering construction costs, interest on capital, profits and selling prices.

While such efforts help us to formulate our ideas of what ought to be, and while a start has been made toward providing public supervision and control, we have yet to see a definite adequate concrete achievement. The " country club district," developed by Mr. Nichols in Kansas City, and Roland Park in Baltimore are among the admirable private efforts, but they are high-class residential neighborhoods. Forest Hills Gardens, the suburb built for investment purposes by the Russell Sage Foundation, is valuable as showing what can be done for middle-class or more prosperous residents, but almost unfortunate in the impression that has spread throughout the country that it shows " how to house the masses."

Groups of suburban house-seekers have joined together to plan coöperative neighborhood development. Such a scheme is being worked out in a beautiful little valley in the environs of Philadelphia by a colony of artists, architects, writers and other professional men and women.

At Akron, Ohio, a tract of four hundred acres two and one-half miles from the business center and one-quarter mile from the plant of the Goodyear Tire and Rubber Company is being developed as a whole by that concern to provide good housing for its employees.

The latter have been consulted at each step in the undertaking.

The development was planned by Warren H. Manning, landscape designer, with special reference to its becoming a part of the city of Akron. Lots are all 50 feet wide and the depth of 110 to 125 feet allows space for gardens. Various restrictions have been imposed. The value of house and lot ranges from $2,000 to $3,000 and the system of payment, which gives ownership in about fifteen years, has a special provision designed to prevent speculation.

The English garden suburbs and first garden city of Letchworth and the English co-partnership tenants' associations, are most suggestive of possible success for America. These have been so often described that it is scarcely necessary here to do more than restate their essentials, indicate their extent, and point out their recent application to the needs of low-paid workingmen, following their success as worked out by middle-class people on moderate salaries and artisans earning good wages.

The fundamental element making for success in both the garden suburbs and the first garden city of Letchworth is collective planning, development and control. The garden suburbs provide dwellings and neighborhood social facilities, such as schools, playgrounds and other recreation features, churches, stores, club buildings and halls. But Letchworth goes further. In addition to all these needs for *living*, it provides for *livelihood* — not merely through planning

the places for factories and workshops, but through
selecting and actually securing the industries best calculated to provide a steady and sufficient economic
basis for the town.

The main principle underlying the Letchworth idea
is that of preserving ultimately for the inhabitants as
a municipality the benefits of the increased value of
the land it owns.   But the essential feature of the co-
partnership tenants' associations is the collective ownership of houses and the sharing of profits with tenants.   A portion of Letchworth is rented by a co-
partnership tenants' association, which is thus applying to about one-tenth of the area of the city the principle of co-partnership in housing.

Each member of a co-partnership tenants' association is a shareholder in it rather than the holder of
a title to a particular house and lot.   The capital is
provided partly from outsiders interested in the success of the undertaking and so content with interest
of 4 or 4½ per cent.   But each tenant member of the
association invests a small sum to begin with and un-
dertakes to increase it gradually, his shares paying 5
per cent.   The tenant's advantages have been summarized by Henry Vivian, member of Parliament and
chairman of the co-partnership tenants' organization,
substantially as follows:

He gets a good house in attractive surroundings for
a rent no higher than he would have to pay elsewhere.
Should values go up he gets the benefit either in a dividend or rent. He secures practically all the surplus

profits after fixed charges have been met. He secures a social atmosphere which awakens new interests, and creates a collective friendship unknown under the individual system of ownership. He secures freedom from loss, should circumstances require him to leave the neighborhood. The capital for building his house is provided at a cheaper rate than it could be obtained on any other system that is commercially sound.

The tenants as a whole can relieve themselves of dependence on outside capital altogether by acquiring through investment or by accumulated capital the value of the property. By a gradual process, therefore, it lies with the tenants to transfer the ownership from non-tenant shareholders, who take the main risk to begin with, to the tenant shareholders who, it is hoped, may become the ultimate owners. The personal interest of the tenant in the prosperity of the community is secured, with a minimum of obstacles to the mobility of his labor and capital.

From a small beginning this co-partnership tenants' movement has grown remarkably in ten years. It now includes fourteen societies with successful developments. The cost value of land and buildings of the federated societies was only $49,844 in 1903; in 1913 it had mounted to $6,782,648. When the present building operations are completed, for which further investments are required, the total value of the estates will be nearly $16,000,000. Houses for artisans have been developed especially by the garden city tenants at Letchworth, where woodworkers, joiners, motor-car makers and printers are numerous in the membership;

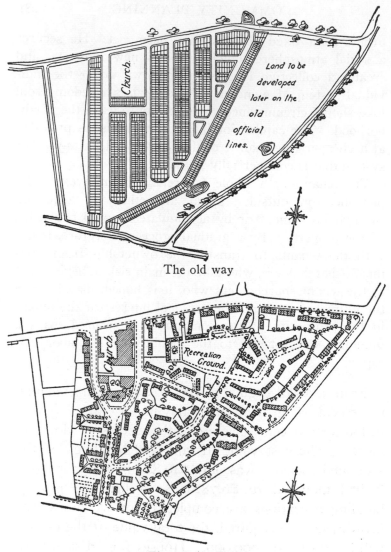

The old way

The modern way

THE NEW PLANNING FOR RESIDENTIAL AREAS ON THE OUTSKIRTS
OF ENGLISH CITIES
From " Practical Town Planning," by J. S. Nettlefold.

by the Harborne Tenants whose members are workers employed in the various trades in Birmingham; and the Stoke-on-Trent Tenants, many of whom are workers in potteries. Two new societies will provide for still lower paid workingmen: The Sealand Tenants for the workers in a large iron works near Chester; and a society which is laying out an estate for the miners near Wrexham. Low rentals of houses already built are shown by the following table:

Houses		Rents	
544 below	$1.50 a week	or	$ 78.00 a year
731 at	$1.50–$2.00 a week or	$ 78.00–	104.00 a year
751 at	2.00– 2.50 a week or	104.00–	130.00 a year
657 at	2.50– 3.00 a week or	130.00–	156.00 a year
151 at	3.00– 3.75 a week or	156.00–	195.00 a year
110 at	3.75– 5.00 a week or	195.00–	260.00 a year
199 over	5.00 a week or		260.00 a year

3,143

Even allowing for the difference in purchasing power in England and the United States, these figures are sufficiently low to challenge our earnest attention in this country.

To what extent are the principles and methods of the English co-partnership garden suburbs and cities adaptable to America?

Many of the factors of economy which make low rents possible there are just as applicable here. Take, for example, collective buying and manufacturing. The federated co-partnership tenants' societies send an agent to Norway to contract for all the lumber needed for their combined developments covering a year. Is not this paralleled in the purchase of supplies by every great combination of manufacturing plants in this country? At Letchworth, this federation has established its own woodworking mill and other shops to manufacture the materials for its building operations throughout England. Does this differ from the practice of our large industrial concerns which often operate their own printing establishments, box factories and the like both for convenience and to save contractors' profits? Again, is there any reason why the scientific study of the function and width of streets, which has brought down the expense of street improvements in these foreign developments, should fail to accomplish a similar lowering of such costs in this country?

It is true that American workingmen have not had much experience in coöperative methods as compared with British and German workingmen. But it is equally true that the only way to gain experience in coöperative methods is by undertaking to practice them. Trade unions and other organizations are teaching them group effort for a given end. The management of tuberculosis sanatoria, homes for the aged and crippled, and similar institutions has been successfully carried on for some time by printers, cigarmakers and railway workers.

The spirit of individual enterprise and "American independence" is thought to be characteristic of middle-class business and professional men, yet the readiness with which they have yielded individual interest to neighborhood welfare is convincingly shown by their acceptance of the restrictions imposed in the residential area developed by Mr. Nichols in Kansas City. It is an easy step further, and an easier one, it would seem, for working people, to accomplish similar and greater results through associations in whose affairs they might have voice and vote.

Pride in individual home ownership may be urged as an American factor which would prevent a hearty acceptance of the principle of co-partnership ownership. Yet the country where this principle has taken such vigorous root is the one where that pride has been supposed to be the strongest — where the boast has been that " every Englishman's home is his castle."

What is needed most urgently in America to-day is a consciousness among the citizens of their stake in the whole community. We have seen how an improved housing scheme in Cincinnati suburbs is designed to make the workingman home buyer also a landlord through selling him a house with two flats, one of which he rents. This establishes the selfish stake in the individual lot and house — the very thing which has so often proved most prejudicial to the proper development of a neighborhood. The co-partnership principle, while encouraging pride and effort in improving the house in which he dwells, gives every man a large interest in the whole neighborhood. The question is: Shall we develop civic spirit on a building lot or on a community scale?

The greater mobility of labor assured by the co-partnership system is both an advantage and a disadvantage under American conditions. If a tenant member of a co-partnership society in Birmingham, for example, is offered a better position in another city, he does not face the handicap which confronts an individual home-owner. He is not forced to sell quickly, which so often means a loss, nor does he have the difficulty and expense of managing his property from his new and distant home. The tenants' society assumes all the burden. His shares in the tenants' society will still bring dividends or the society will buy back his shares, which will help to establish his new home. Perhaps he will find there another co-partnership tenants' association which he can join.

Would not sudden defection of many tenants ruin an association? The writer asked this question when visiting the Harborne tenants' estate at Birmingham. The secretary replied in the negative and took from his safe a convincing document. It was a list of several hundred applicants who were on the waiting list for the Harborne dwellings. "If every house on the estate were to become vacant to-morrow," he said, "we could fill them up in three weeks." This is assured, of course, in the co-partnership garden suburbs by the very fact that they are suburbs and can thus draw on a large city's population. In the case of Letchworth,

STREETS IN HARBORNE, CO-PARTNERSHIP SUBURB, BIRMINGHAM,
ENGLAND

it has been the design to give stability — as already described — through diversity of industries.

Mobility of labor is admittedly greater in America than in England. Our fluctuations are often sudden and large. From this point of view, co-partnership tenants' associations and estates would therefore seem to be even more desirable to the American than to the English workingman. They would give him practically all the advantages of home ownership while not making a particular house a millstone around his neck or a means of putting him at the mercy of his employer. But this relative freedom to move might prove a serious handicap to the success of such associations in this country. It may well be asked whether the English associations would have been so successful without a strong permanent nucleus of tenants on each estate.

Much can be said against any factor in American life tending to increase a mobility which even now is perhaps a detriment to the stability and public spirit of our communities. But the co-partnership estates in England, while leaving the tenant free to move, provide, as Mr. Vivian points out, attractive surroundings and neighborly spirit which in themselves strengthen the desire of the tenant to remain. This is lacking in almost every American industrial town. We might well gain, by the introduction of the co-partnership principle, both a free scope for our mobility and a strong legitimate incentive to permanence of residence.

The difficulties of success in starting and conducting co-operative effort is increased in this country by our heterogeneous population. But careful selection of the places and the groups for the pioneer schemes would minimize this handicap.

The experience of many paternalistic housing schemes in this country shows that, along with wholesome, attractive dwellings and the economic advantages of low rents, there are sociological factors which are essential to the highest success. Autocratic control is now generally dismissed from consideration. Failure to provide for recreation and social life has impaired the success of many housing efforts which were otherwise carefully planned. Has not the lack of social control by the tenants been another handicap? If we now admit that facilities for *community* life are essential, does that not indicate that we may have discounted too much the social instincts and spirit of our fellow-citizens? May not this very desire for *community* life indicate that people are more nea ly ready than we suspect for coöperative effort?

Among the housing reformers who are public-spirited enough to be content with "philanthropy and 5 per cent.," may we not find capital at the same rate of interest for co-partnership undertakings? May not the public spirit of English business men who have given liberally of their experience and energy toward putting the co-partnership tenants' associations on a sound basis, find a parallel in America?

The managers of industrial corporations are vitally interested in good housing for their employees, both as a factor in health, which means efficient work-people, and as a means of assuring a stable working force. But most of them are convinced that the rôles of landlord and employer should not be combined. The industrial concerns which wish to use surplus funds in housing schemes might apply them through an organization formed to stimulate tenants' associations.

The building and loan associations of the United States give some indication of the extent to which home-building utilizes the savings not only of those who are building houses but of small investors. According to a recent report of the secretary of the United States League of Building and Loan Associations, there were in 1911, 6,429 associations having 2,836,433 members, and total assets of $1,248,479,139. The average amount due each member was about $440 as compared with about $430, the average amount credited to each depositor in the savings banks. The regulations of a typical society provide: " That an investment of $5,000 is the largest accepted from any one individual; the dividend rate is 4½ per cent. per annum and withdrawals are, during ordinary times, paid on demand; loans are on first mortgages only, in amounts never exceeding $10,000 on one security and they are made within a radius of twenty-five miles from the society's headquarters."

This billion of dollars is certainly not a negligible factor in considering the possibilities of co-partnership tenants' associations. Indeed the point has already been well discussed before the league by a former president, Julius Stern of the Chicago bar, who had visited the garden suburbs of England. At a recent convention of the league he said,

The aim of the American associations hitherto may be summarized as the encouragement of habits of thrift by systematic economy and the accumulation, by the co-operation of many members, of a fund to be loaned to the coöperators in turn, upon a mortgage secured by a homestead, bought or built by the borrower; and the gradual extinguishment of the mortgage by regular, continued periodic payments, in moderate installments.

The conditions of congestion and overcrowding confronting the cities of this country, as well as of Europe, must be met here as there; and what appears to be the happiest solution for these conditions, and one with which it seems to me the building associations are here best fitted to cope, if they will adapt themselves to the work, is that presented by the garden city and garden suburbs movement which was started in England a few years ago.

After describing the suburbs of the English co-partnership tenants' associations, he went on to say:

This movement aims at the creation of real homes, each family under its own roof-tree surrounded by ample grounds with plenty of light, air and the opportunity for healthful exercise in gardening during leisure hours, with its residential character protected against invasion and a collective interest in the advancing values of the communal ground.

The work of our members in the past has been largely

along utilitarian lines and has been so far well done. We have arrived at a point where an enlarged horizon lies before us and higher ethical ideals must outline our further progress. By collective undertakings in the future, we may surpass the achievements gained by individual efforts in the past, in securing not only homes that are a shelter, but homes that shall embody all the elements, physical, esthetic and moral, that the word " home " implies, with more of beauty within, more of protection from without, and achieved with greater economy than before.

In order that we may avail ourselves of the benefits of this movement, and substitute our corporate action in fathering garden city projects, in place of the individual action of subdividing promoters, we must doubtless devise and obtain legislation permitting our associations to so broaden the sphere of their activities as to become purchasers of lands and builders of houses, or possibly to act in conjunction with auxiliary bodies upon which these functions might devolve; but judging from the extended powers which have of recent years been granted in some of the states to the building and loan associations, permitting them to accept deposits, issue certificates, borrow moneys, and lend moneys to one another, we may fairly anticipate the obtaining of further privileges when the legislators can be shown that the objects are purely coöperative, the results so beneficial, and the investment so safely secured as has been demonstrated by the existing experimental cities abroad.

A committee of the league was appointed to study the matter.

The effort to establish the co-partnership housing

The Park

Public Neighborhood Hall

COMMUNITY FACILITIES AT HARBORNE CO-PARTNERSHIP GARDEN
SUBURB, BIRMINGHAM, ENGLAND

293

principle has already been started in America. The Massachusetts Homestead Commission has planned for its application to a development in that state. A site has been selected at North Billerica, twenty-seven miles from Boston. At Billerica the repair shops of the Boston and Maine Railroad, employing one thousand two hundred men, were recently located. These workmen, and the shop officials as well, are in need of good housing, and both have been interested in the project.

A beautiful tract of fifty-seven acres has been secured along the Concord River at a cost far below that demanded by real-estate operators for less attractive land farther from the shops. The plans provide for a portion of the area to be developed by a co-partnership society. Another section is for houses to be sold outright on installments, each owner taking up 10 per cent. of value in stock. In a third section the plan is to build houses for rent, and in a fourth the company expects to construct special buildings as the demand arises for shops, lodging, boarding houses, etc. The city planner of the scheme, Arthur C. Comey, a member of the Homestead Commission, writes:

Briefly stated the company proposes to solve permanently the increasingly difficult housing problem on the areas under its control — by elimination of speculative profits, distributing the payments for the home, wholesale operations, constructing houses of durable materials, limiting the number of houses per acre, scientific planning along advanced garden suburb lines, providing community buildings and playgrounds, laying out allotment gardens, and promoting the formation of a co-partnership society.

Another development planned in Massachusetts is the proposed Neponsit Garden Village at Walpole where the paper factory of C. S. Bird and Sons is located. This plan is in the hands of John Nolen, and it is expected that a portion of the village will be developed by a co-partnership society, the formation of which is to be encouraged.

When we turn to the exercise of public authority in guiding city growth, Canada and the United States have both begun to apply the principle of the British Housing and Town Planning Act. This legislation, enacted in 1909, is nothing less than epoch-making. It extends government supervision, control and guidance to the development of residential additions and city expansion. Under it, town planning schemes may, subject to the approval of the Local Government Board, be prepared by the local authority or the landowners "as respects any land likely to be used for building purposes" or any neighboring land. A way is provided under the Local Government Board for giving proper consideration and adjustment to objections. On the other hand, landowners whose schemes have failed of adoption by the local authorities may appeal to the Board. And the Board, if satisfied that local authorities have failed to take the requisite steps for a town planning scheme, may order one to be prepared. The Board is also given large power to prescribe the provisions of town planning schemes and limit the number of houses per acre.

The significance of this legislation can scarcely be overestimated. It made community interests paramount through the exercise of public authority which had prior to 1909 been largely at the mercy of the landowners. The act thus establishes a most important principle and a method. But under it and the regulations drawn up by the Local Government Board the town planning procedure is in some ways cumbersome.

This was to be expected in the application of completely new legislation. John S. Nettlefold of Birmingham has pointed out in his " Practical Town Planning " that too much was left by Parliament in the hands of the Local Government Board without first making sure that the Board understood the work and had the time to attend to it. He has suggested amendments to the act to simplify procedure, to remove some of the seven opportunities property owners have to object to a town planning scheme before the scheme is finally authorized by the Board, to make the act apply to existing towns as well as undeveloped districts, to reduce the exorbitant prices which are paid for land for public purposes, and to provide an adequate supply of cheap capital for approved housing schemes.

The defects which have cropped out naturally in the operation of the law will doubtless be remedied and do not in any way detract from the fundamental importance of the new policy which the act inaugurates in England and suggests for America.

On this side of the water, Ontario has adopted a city and suburbs plans act." Plans for subdividing an area within five miles of a city of 50,000 or more must be submitted to the Ontario Railway and Municipal Board, which is thus given a position corresponding in some degree to that of the Local Government Board under the British Act. This Railway and Municipal Board may require changes in the plan to make it accord with any general scheme the city may have adopted. There is provision for hearings, should a city object to any plan proposed by the landowners, before the Board can give its approval.

The Ontario act was hailed by the *Canadian Municipal Journal* as "a great advance in municipal planning," whose provisions "will prevent the unreasonable plans which real-estate speculators have been in the habit of providing outside city limits. . . . Fortunately in Ontario such over riding of public rights by private whims is now stopped." The legislature of New Brunswick has also passed a town planning act along similar lines.

In our own country some degree of control over the platting of outlying land has been given to cities in Michigan, Pennsylvania, Massachusetts, Connecticut, New Jersey and Wisconsin. In the latter state this authority extends to all territory within a mile and a half of the city boundary, and in Michigan to land within three miles of the limits of the municipality.

Under legislation enacted recently, Massachusetts cities and towns of more than 10,000 population are authorized and directed to create a local planning board not only to plan for the future but to study the present situation. These boards will make social surveys of their communities and use the information not only to guide town planning but to remedy existing evils. All the work of the local boards will be carried on under the general supervision of the Massachusetts Homestead Commission.

A bill was passed by the New York State legislature giving cities and villages power to appoint planning commissions, with authority, however, only to investigate and report. On a few matters other bodies may be required to suspend action until after such reports are received. In a score of other states city planning legislation of one sort or another is being considered.

The Pennsylvania legislature recently authorized city planning commissions for second-class cities — Pittsburgh and Scranton — with power to recommend new streets and highways, changes in existing ones and locations for public buildings, play-grounds, boulevards and civic centers. All plots or replots of land laid out for residential subdivisions are to be submitted to it for approval before they can be recorded. These commissions were given recommendatory power to plot new streets three miles beyond the city's limits. Similar legislation was passed applying to cities of the third class.

Another law enacted by the Pennsylvania legislature made provision for the creation of a "metropolitan planning district" embracing the territory within twenty-five miles beyond the limits of Philadelphia. By the terms of this measure each district was authorized to have a "metropolitan planning commission" on which either directly or indirectly, each political unit in the district was to be represented. Each commission was directed to plan for its metropolitan area such facilities of common concern as water, sewage disposal, main highways and park systems. The act was found to be inconsistent with a phrase in the state constitution, so that its repeal became necessary pending efforts to secure a constitutional amendment.

The example, of course, for this sort of collective action by a group of cities and towns is to be found in the commission government of Boston's metropolitan district. Some of the advocates of this legislation feel that through it better results can be secured than through the annexation of suburbs. It is a fair question whether the advantages claimed for local autonomy — that some things can be done better by the progressive small community than by the big unwieldy city, and that local loyalties are worth conserving — outweigh the disadvantages when one laggard small community obstructs the best interests of the group as a whole. The problem is not dissimilar to that involved in getting uniform legislation in several states. Even under the group action of metropolitan commissions, the inclination to shirk a part in the responsibilities of the district as a whole, while sharing the advantages of the proximity to a larger city, has been very clearly manifest in the attitude of Brookline and many another suburb which has fought annexation.

The principle and purpose underlying the British Town Planning Act and the first steps toward similar legislation in America, are an inspiring challenge to the new types of public officials, broadminded employers, capitalists and citizens devoted to the promotion of public welfare.

The importance and significance of the problems with which these chapters have dealt are increasingly apparent. An appendix presents brief discussions by several contributors whose thought and efforts have been applied to the subject in such a way as to give their words authority.

The great need is for demonstration and example. Study and discussion concerning our own conditions and experience and the efforts abroad have already been sufficient to warrant a concrete undertaking. A successful achievement in the form of a garden suburb or city, meeting the needs of an industrial population, and assuring to the community as a whole the increase of land values, would go farther than any other one thing to give point and effectiveness and stimulus to the movement for better cities and neighborhoods in which so many of us have to live.

Such an achievement would not only set the example for similar developments, but would serve the still more important purpose of encouraging the guidance of all city growth through intelligent town planning legislation administered by competent public authority. Our city planners have the problem in hand. There is needed the effort of those who take satisfaction in "philanthropy and 5 per cent."; the loan of public funds at low interest; the help of industrial captains who are already finding removal from congestion so profitable, and who seek efficient workers through giving them a chance for escape from crowded tenements; the enlistment of the organizations which already have done so much to help the people of this country secure homes; and the coöperation of all these groups and interests with progressive public officials and those who seek only the chance for a wholesome life. It is to be hoped that we shall soon see an embodiment on our own soil of that which, in the English Letchworth, is giving reality to a vision — the vision of a sane and simple extension of democracy from the realm of politics into the affairs of industry and everyday life.

APPENDIX

SATELLITE CITIES FROM VARIOUS VIEWPOINTS

THE HUMAN EMPHASIS

By

CHARLES MULFORD ROBINSON

Author of "Modern Municipal Art" and "Width and Arrangement of Streets: A Study in Town Planning"

IN THE discussion of the establishment of industrial plants on the outskirts of the city, we have heard much regarding such economic factors as cheaper land, lower taxes, room for expansion, better lighted buildings and the possible greater convenience of transportation facilities; but we have not heretofore heard enough about the human factor. This, since it represents labor, is, however, one of the most important elements in causing economic success or failure. If better living conditions and contentment shall give efficiency and stability to employees who live near suburban factories, the "satellite city" will have economically justified itself and will succeed. If these results do not follow, the city will not succeed.

Two reasons may prevent the desired results. Employees may not find the better conditions anticipated, or they may fail to move with the factory and give a trial to the conditions. Indicative of the latter possibility were the statistics showing the percentage of work-

ers at Norwood and Oakley who still live in downtown
Cincinnati — 44.68, not to mention those in other sections who live so far from their work as also to suffer
loss of time, of money, of energy and perhaps of health
in daily railroad travel between their homes and the Norwood and Oakley workshops. As has been shown, this
anomalous condition created social and operative problems involving expense to employers as well as to employees.

Now, in removing labor to the outskirts of cities, there
is a degree of inertia, a doubting conservatism and a
habit to be overcome which need the allurement of advantages as unmistakable as those which are required to
move the factory itself. And it should be clear that
these advantages cannot be secured if there be failure
to plan in advance the location and character of streets,
and thus of lots, for to fail to plan these is to leave the
employee at the mercy of land speculators. If he moves,
conditions are little better than they were before; and
in a great many cases he will fortunately foresee this outcome and decline to move. Either result must mean the
sociological, and ultimately the economic, failure of the
satellite city. It is of great value to give to this point,
by means of examples good and bad, the emphasis it
ought to have.

THE WAY OUT
By
GEORGE B. FORD
City Planning Lecturer at Columbia University

In a consideration of industrial suburbs there stand
out two vital facts: first, The betterment of the working-

man's living conditions can come only through the workingman himself; second, An immense amount of discomfort, dreariness, unsanitariness and waste in workingmen's communities could have been avoided by the early application of scientific city planning.

Employers' welfare work has never proved really successful. Even in the best examples there is a certain underlying current of writhing under paternalism due to pride in American democracy, which causes the workingman to resent having his pabulum thrust down to him.

The big corporations and the lenders of money are telling employers who think of providing better housing, etc., for their employees that it is most inadvisable. The result is that there has been very little done along these lines for the past year or two.

The next choice is for the employee to submit himself to the tender mercies of the speculative land operator and builder. We all know very well whose interest is being served in this case.

The third and only remaining choice is for the workingman to look out for himself. Singly, he is at a great disadvantage from lack of experience and because most things cost more in detail than they do in large quantities.

Therefore, it is obvious that the only effective solution of the problem is coöperative action on the part of workingmen. Just what form this coöperative action should take can be decided only by experiment though we have a splendid point of departure in the most successful English co-partnership suburbs.

As to the medium through which such coöperative action can be taken it is evident that if something along this line already exists which has the confidence and support of the workingman, advantage should be taken of it. In looking over the field for such a medium, one organization stands prominently before all others, the league of building and loan associations. The United States League of Building and Loan Associations represents a total invested capital of over $1,000,000,000 and represents over 2,500,000 members. Its power is tremendous and it does have the confidence of the workingman. This organization has been considering the housing problem. A plan of action will soon be forthcoming. The possibilities in such a movement are enormous.

Large cities are spending millions to-day to widen streets, cut through new streets, provide parks and playgrounds in congested areas, almost all of which might have been saved if the city had been originally planned with foresight. Hundreds of millions are spent on hospitals, asylums, sanatoria, jails, health, police and fire departments, a large portion of which could have been saved if the cities had not been so wastefully and unscientifically designed.

For example, if the lot and block units and dimensions in sections surrounding the factories which moved to Norwood and Oakley, on the outskirts of Cincinnati, had been laid out along lines which experience has shown to be most economical and desirable for workingmen's dwellings and if provision had been made for recreation for grown-ups as well as for children as suggested by the English garden suburbs, the neighborhood of the factories would now be almost exclusively occupied by the employees in those factories instead of largely by clerks and business men who commute daily to Cincinnati. And furthermore, the slum problem of Cincinnati itself would be vastly less urgent. If the lots were cut for the occupant instead of the occupant being trimmed to the lot; if streets and roadways were designed in location, direction, character and width for use and not according to obsolete precedent; if transit lines were designed with the same efficiency that the manufacturer exhibits in designing his own plant; if people could only realize that money spent in scientifically designed recreational facilities is paid back in many ways to the community, then the workingmen's residential area, instead of being an eyesore and a disgrace to the community, would be what the English garden suburbs now are, the most charming and efficient housing areas to be found anywhere in the world.

The problem is simple. It requires first, merely an appreciation of the fact that city planning pays; and second, it requires a coöperative effort on the part of the workingmen to secure such scientific city planning.

It can be done and we are confident that the next few years will prove it beyond all question of doubt so that even the blindest will see.

CO PARTNERSHIP HOUSING
By
HENRY VIVIAN, M.P.
Chairman Co-Partnership Tenants, Ltd., England

The trend of population from cities to new areas on the outskirts is good for the individual and the nation, provided the suburbs are planned with a view to the development of a healthy people. But unless care is taken at the outset and a standard of housing maintained, many of the new districts will degenerate into the condition of congested areas as we know them to-day.

It is not enough to devise rows of houses along geometrically planned streets; such monotony of outlook is almost as depressing as life in a crowded city tenement. As the leisure hours of the people increase the organization of their pleasures will become as important as the utilization of their working day. And if spare time is to be spent near the home, the home must be placed in surroundings that give it a magnetic quality for the wage-earner.

In England we find that better health and mental vigor of the workers are a result of the garden suburb movement, notably in the case of printers, carpenters and others who have left London to work in the co-partnership factories at the garden city of Letchworth. None can question the advantages of a good natural environment over the squalid surroundings that are too often the lot of the workingman.

But observations on conditions in industrial suburbs bring out a further point of importance, viz., that "house ownership may often be a very doubtful advantage to the workingman." It may hamper his mobility when opportunity for advancement offers elsewhere, and it is often risky as well as expensive for workmen to try to buy, on the usual individualistic plan, the houses in which they live. Assuming that an estate has been laid out and houses built in a satisfactory way, the system of ownership and administration determines whether the value of a good beginning is realized by the community.

If sites and houses are sold to individual purchasers without adequate restrictions, the chances are that some of these will soon part with their property to undesirable people, who will use it in such a way as to frustrate the good intentions of those who laid out the estate.

If one or two houses in a street pass into the permanent ownership of undesirables, who rack-rent and otherwise misuse the property, the value of the whole street rapidly diminishes. The system which encourages the workman to buy his own house, but creates no interest on the part of the residents in keeping up the character of a neighborhood as a whole makes no provision for dealing with such evils.

Co-partnership in housing, which is now developing in various parts of England, is giving the sense of ownership to the tenants without the disadvantages of the individualistic system. The policy of admitting tenants to participate in the profits of an estate and enabling them to become investors in its capital seems to meet the situation better than any other plan yet devised. It gives them the educational advantage and stimulus to economy which arises from a sense of individual ownership, combined with safeguards to prevent such ownership expressing itself in an anti-social direction. On these estates facilities for open-air recreation, indoor social pleasures and the delights of gardening interests are enjoyed in common. The limitation of the number of houses to the acre and the provision of ample open spaces secure for town-dwellers new interest in life and give children a chance for healthy development.

The experience gained in this movement proves that it is to the interest of the whole nation that the areas on which people are to live shall previously be planned to prevent a reversion to the old evils. Moreover, the fresher outlook and keener vigor associated with men living on estates thus planned is a considerable factor in the national efficiency. In other words, the long view in housing is the best security for the future.

We need to limit not only the number of houses per acre, but also the number of persons per house. The injury to health of overcrowding has been demonstrated again and again, but the facts recently brought to light by Maxwell Henderson, medical officer of health for Edinburgh, will be new to American readers. Mr. Henderson had the city divided into its different wards and compared the relationship of the death rate with the number of one- and two-roomed houses in each ward. The following table shows the result of his inquiry:

Ward.	Deaths per 1,000.	No. of 1 and 2 roomed houses.
St. Bernard's	7	739
St. Andrew's	9	1,315
Calton	10	1,715
Gorgie	11	2,225
Dalry	11	3,332
George Square	13	5,462
St. Leonard's	13	3,731
Canongate	14	2,699
St. Giles	15	6,978

Dr. Andrew, the Medical Officer of Health for Hendon (the Urban District in which the Hampstead Garden Suburb is situated), gives some interesting figures in his report for 1913. The gross death rate for the whole of his district is 11.74 per 1,000; for the suburb the rate is 6.54: the rate for England and Wales is 13.4. The particulars of infant mortality are equally striking: the rate for the Hendon District is 85 per 1,000; for the suburb, 40; for England and Wales, 109.

In this connection it seems clear:

1. That badly arranged tenements, congested populations existing in them, and an undue density of popula-

tion per acre go hand in hand with an increase in the death and sickness rates.

2. That the subdivision of dwelling houses with a view to creating an increased number of a smaller description, contributes towards the foregoing evils and should be rigorously prevented.

3. That while tenement dwelling houses may be provided in cities for sections of the community, the height of these and the number of persons which each is capable of accommodating are matters which call for increased supervision and, if necessary, legislation.

4. That a well-arranged colony system of dwelling is highly preferable and certainly immeasurably more healthful, and that, therefore, where possible such buildings should be erected in preference to tenements.

5. That the existence and spread of tuberculosis has an unquestionable connection with and bearing upon the class of dwelling houses, and that the supervision of suitable housing accommodations should be regarded as the primary step in future efforts to effectually deal with this disease.

FACTORS IN PLANT EFFICIENCY

By

IRVING T. BUSH

President Bush Terminal Company, New York

The industrial success of any community ultimately depends upon facilities for the economical shipping and receiving of freight. Labor conditions do not differ materially in competing centers, and it is possible to create modern factory buildings about as well in one location as in another. The difficult problem is that of shipping and receiving freight. In the older cities, industrial locations were chosen without reference to a railroad siding. Competition with newer communities, where factories were located directly adjoining railroads, has placed the older cities at a disadvantage, and modern competition is so keen that the cost of carting the crude material from the railroad to the factory, and the finished product from the factory to the railroad, is, in many cases, the difference between profit and loss. It is not sufficient to secure a location upon one railroad. Adequate facilities require a location upon all the railroads serving a given center.

.Older communities, while at a disadvantage from the standpoint of rail facilities, possess many other advantages which newer communities cannot duplicate. Existing cities should strive to maintain their advantages and to create conditions which will overcome their shipping disadvantages. To do this, they must either bring the railroad car to the factory, or take the factory to the railroad car. In many of the great cities, it is obviously impossible to do the former. The solution seems to be to create union manufacturing centers just outside of the congested area, where the cars of all of the railroads can serve the industries there located. This arrangement not only protects the industrial welfare of the community adopting it, but lessens the congestion in the city streets, for instead of uselessly hauling back and forth between the railroad station and the shipping-room the crude and manufactured product, only such portion of the finished product as is required for actual consumption within the congested area is hauled through the city streets.

Industrial centers of this kind, on the outskirts of great cities, are built on the sound principle of the elimination of unnecessary effort. If this principle is successfully carried out the industries will flourish. Labor will follow the industry, and a fortunate by-product result in the bettering of the home conditions of the laborer by moving him away from the congested area into better living conditions.

PLANNING FOR METROPOLITAN NEEDS
By
ANDREW WRIGHT CRAWFORD
*Secretary City Parks Association, Philadelphia; Member
Executive Committee National Conference on City Planning*

We are beginning to appreciate the necessity of making our city plans coëxtensive with the community that uses the city and of providing for social needs in the enlarged sphere. By "city community" I mean the community marked, not by arbitrary legal limits, but by the daily ebb and flow of the population, whether that movement is the customary one from the suburbs to the center of the city in the morning and vice versa at night, or involves also the reverse as is the case in the suburbs of Cincinnati. To this end coöperation must in some way be secured among all the communities within the radius of that ebb and flow — a radius that is apt to be not less than twenty-five miles in extent — or else annexation and consolidation must follow.

Personally, I believe that in most of the suburban communities of the country annexation is not desired and not desirable. The smaller community can frequently do better for itself in many respects than the enlarged city would do for the district. It is true that Pullman seems to be an example to the contrary but I am inclined to think that this is true because of the mistaken character of Pullman originally, a character that is not typical of other suburban boroughs and towns; hence its example is misleading.

If the metropolitan needs of the community referred to are met by a metropolitan scheme of organization, local matters can be left to local authority. I believe that it is only through metropolitan planning that metropolitan needs can be met and consolidation and annexation postponed. If Boston had not conceived the idea of its Metropolitan Sewer Commission, its Metropolitan Water Commission, its Metropolitan Park Commission, the thirty-eight communities within the metropolitan area would by this time have been compelled to come under one city government.

By "metropolitan planning needs" I refer, for instance, to the sewer system, the sewage disposal system, the water system, the main highway system, the park system, and other community needs upon which joint action could advantageously be secured.

The sewer systems of certain political units adjacent to Philadelphia naturally drain into its sewer system. There should be one sewage disposal plant for these political units. If they had some method by which the cost of a single plant could be divided among them, I am sure they would all coöperate readily, but as yet there is no such provision.

Thoroughfares should be continuous. A man wants to go from one point to another regardless of whether he crosses one or five or twenty-five governmental units; it makes no difference to him in his immediate work, nor to the community. What is wanted are direct thoroughfares.

The water system naturally should be one system.

The park system should likewise be one. While it is desirable to preserve for park purposes the beautiful valleys near Philadelphia, the desirability is increased five-fold if they are to constitute one continuous park connection for several governmental units.

There is need of planning for the metropolitan area, an area of twenty or twenty-five miles radius. The same need has been felt in other cities. For example, Boston has created three metropolitan commissions, for water, sewage and parks, and a preliminary commission on highways. Pittsburgh feels the need of adopting the metropolitan district idea.

This recognition is not confined to the United States. An article by the city engineer of Liverpool, complains of the fact that the local boards outside of Liverpool do not coöperate as they should to put through metropolitan schemes, and he points out the difficulties. At the Conference on Destitution which met some time ago in London, Charles C. Reade, editor of the New Zealand *Graphic* and a delegate from Australia, declared:

"There is a conspicuous and characteristic problem before, not only Sydney, but all the Australasian cities, and that is the proper control and direction of their suburban areas. It is somewhat remarkable that whilst the central areas have been consciously planned and laid out on a scale far superior to many older English cities, whilst the concrete example of civic orderliness is before them, the suburbs have been permitted to grow in haphazard fashion. This is well illustrated by the case of Auckland, a conspicuous example of what rapid development, land speculation, and municipal failure to control the growth is producing in the newer suburban districts of Australasian cities. The fundamental difficulty which faces them all is the existence of numerous local bodies within the metropolitan area. In Auckland, for instance, there are sixteen, Adelaide has nineteen, Melbourne twenty-two, and Sydney no less than forty-two. The confines of these cities are frequently in the hands of bodies that correspond in character to the English urban district councils. There is no cohesion or comprehensive system for seeing that new roads or ' estates ' are so planned as to fit into and become an integral part in the design of the cities as a whole."

The question is one that affects every metropolitan city in the world. The efforts to grapple with it in Pennsylvania were initiated in Philadelphia, where there was recently held a Suburban Planning Conference to which representatives of the 132 governmental units within twenty-five miles of Philadelphia were invited. As a result, a bill was passed by the Pennsylvania Legislature creating suburban metropolitan districts embracing areas of twenty-five miles radius beyond the limits of cities of the first class — Philadelphia being the only one. Owing to an unfortunate phrase in the state constitution this act has since been repealed, pending a constitutional amendment. The measure provided for the creation of a commission authorized to plan for the metropolitan needs of the district, and formulate plans covering any particular need brought to its attention by any one of the governmental units embraced in the district. Reports with recommendations were to be submitted by the commission each year to each of the governmental units. These were to be followed in so far as each such unit should decide. This metropolitan planning measure followed a law enacted recently creating city planning commissions in cities of the second class. All plotting of land in such a city and within three miles beyond its limits must be approved by the commission, which also has power to make recommendations concerning the laying out and development of land in this area.

Good plans, brought forward by a responsible body and published broadcast so that people know them, do get carried out. What further legislation may be necessary in the future we cannot now predict, but I believe that the inherent power merely to plan will be of great benefit to these metropolitan areas.

FACTORY AND HOME[1]

By

JOHN NOLEN

Landscape Architect, Cambridge, Mass.

The best sites in which to secure factory efficiency are those which afford cheap land in large unbroken blocks — this means lower investment and a ground floor system of factory construction which permits of well-lighted, ventilated and supervised work-rooms; freight facilities; and advantages in obtaining and holding employees who are well housed at low rates in a good environment. Such locations can best be found or provided on the outskirts of a city.

The more important advantages that would seem to be assured to workmen's homes in the outskirts as against homes in the city are as follows:

[1] Mr. Nolen's contribution is a part of a paper he read at a recent annual conference of the National Housing Association.

Though working entirely independently, with a different approach to the problems and in some respects a very different point of view, Mr. Nolen in his paper gives expression to views and conclusions strikingly similar to many of those in " Satellite Cities."

a. The first and most important is the opportunity for relatively cheap land. It is seldom that a workman can afford a home (house and land) valued higher than $2,000 or $3,000. This would mean a rent equivalent, perhaps, of from $15 to $25 a month or from $180 to $300 a year, and would require probably an income of from $750 to $1,200 a year. On this assumption, the workmen under consideration could scarcely afford to own or occupy land valued at more than from $400 to $600. In the outskirts it would be often possible for this sum to obtain a tenth or an eighth, or even a larger portion of an acre, which would make possible the construction of a satisfactory detached or semi-detached single family home with a garden large enough for pleasure and for profitable cultivation. In the central tenement section of a city this sum invested in land would probably not command more than one-eightieth of an acre.

b. In the outskirts a workman would have the advantage of being near (and yet it should not be too near) his work and the incidental saving of time and carfare. This might amount in a year to as much as $30, equivalent to 5 per cent. interest on $600, just about enough, in fact, to cover the value of his land. Proximity to work in many cases would also permit the workman to return to his home for a hot midday meal or to have such a meal brought to him by some member of his family, a decided advantage from the point of view of health, pleasure and family life.

c. A home in the outskirts would place a workman close to the open, rural country and to the city's outlying larger parks, a situation particularly advantageous for the health, education and recreation of his wife and children.

d. In order that a home in the outskirts may be acceptable to the average workman, two additional advantages are virtually indispensable. First, there should be certain local utilities and facilities, such as pure water, sewers, gas, electricity, well-paved streets and sidewalks, local stores, schools, playgrounds and parks; lodges, churches, saloons (or some satisfactory substitute) ; cheap theaters, refreshment gardens, social centers, etc. The workman, if he is to live happily in the outskirts, with proper use of leisure time, needs a well-planned and well-developed local community, a place that has the attractions of the regulated model factory village or so-called " garden suburb " or " garden city." The successful establishment of such a community requires democratic coöperation, town planning, and, to some extent, numbers. The costs of public utilities and private convenience are heavy for a population of less than 10,000, and a population of 25,-000 can meet them much better.

Second, there should be some convenient and inexpensive means of transportation that will give the workman and his family an opportunity to mingle in the life of the city and to draw upon, occasionally at least, the best in music, art, and drama, common only to big cities. Such a journey usually should not take more than a half-hour's time in electric car or train, nor cost more than a five- or ten-cent fare.

This discussion is not theoretical. Its truth may be tested by reviewing typical examples of factories in built-up sections of American and European cities, and the effect of the location upon the factories themselves. With these should be compared typical examples of factories on the outskirts of cities or in the open country. Then finally the same sort of comparison should be made of workmen's homes — those in central, closely built neighborhoods and those in outlying suburban, rural, or "industrial sections." The comparison of both factories and homes should include tables showing costs for a period of years, and some attempt to gauge the relative efficiency under each system.

Nothing would contribute more to a good understanding of this subject than an open-minded examination and study of existing industrial and housing conditions in the built-up sections of large cities and also in such places in this country as Pullman, Homestead, South Omaha, Chicago Heights, Flint, Erie, Oakley, Norwood, Gary, Fairfield; and in such places abroad as Essen; Hellerau, near Dresden; Thiers, France; Agneta Park, Holland; Serrieres, Switzerland; Port Sunlight, Bourneville, Hampstead, Huddersfield, Trafford Park, Manchester, and Letchworth, England.

The general tentative conclusions from this brief examination of the problem of the factory and the home are five:

1. That new factories for their own interest and in the interest of all concerned should locate in the outskirts of cities whenever practicable;

2. That existing factories in cities should be encouraged, as opportunity offers, to remove to the outskirts;

3. That employers and employees should coöperate in a social and democratic way to create an attractive local community on the outskirts of cities near factories, each doing their part to make the local community healthful, convenient and satisfying;

4. That the same coöperation should be directed toward securing also for employees and their families, by

transportation facilities, some of the advantages and permanent attractions of city life;

5. That the choice for factory employees should not be sharply drawn between the city and the country. Both should be recognized as desirable — the city for occasional inspiration and diversion, and the more open country on the outskirts of cities for the essentials of daily life.

THE EMPLOYERS' PART

By

FLAVEL SHURTLEFF

Secretary National Conference on City Planning

In spite of many lost opportunities of producing in America well-planned industrial towns, we must continue to depend on the enthusiastic coöperation of industrial managers and the considerable outlay of industrial capital for an experiment in city building which cares for the housing of people of small means.

Other investors must count the cost of carrying out a plan; the cost of land and its development; the cost of superintendence; the cost of marketing the lots and of building and renting the houses. In the absence of philanthropic motives they will not be attracted by the ordinary rates of interest on their outlay in an undertaking which requires so much personal supervision. Comfortable homes in attractive surroundings cannot be rented for $10 and $12 a month and show profit enough on the investment to attract ordinary investors. But industrial managers are not or should not be ordinary investors. Up to a certain point, they do not have to count the cost of carrying out generous plans for improving the living conditions of their employees. If such an investment yields an abundant supply of more efficient and more contented workers the return is ample.

There are far-sighted employers with a personal interest in the welfare of their working people, who have done much for their comfort by providing more attractive homes and better opportunities for social relaxation. In many instances their efforts have been limited only by the size of the industry which will not permit the carrying out of ambitious plans.

The opportunity for directors of giant industries is too plain to be emphasized, but to smaller employers is offered the same opportunity through a kind of combination which is safe from prosecution under the Sherman Law. An agreement between several industries to locate in one place and to unite their resources under competent direction for the production of the best possible place to live and work in should enable smaller employers to carry out their most ambitious plans.

There are several precedents which prove such an agreement not entirely Utopian. The removal of many of the factories of Cincinnati to the suburbs of Oakley and Norwood is but one case in point. This removal, however, merely furnished the opportunity. It provided the population for a possible model town. Either because the directors of the industries in Oakley and Norwood were not fully convinced of the advantages of providing an attractive place to live in as well as to work in, or for other reasons, the opportunity was not seized and people worked in the suburbs and to a large extent lived in the slums. Complete the development at Norwood and Oakley by planning for the housing and recreation of the small wage-earner and even by importing a bit of the " bright light " attraction of Cincinnati, and the living conditions of the industrial worker will be revolutionized.

FROM THE HOUSING POINT OF VIEW
By
JOHN IHLDER
Field Secretary National Housing Association

From the housing point of view there is no more hopeful factor in our recent city building than the tendency of industries to move to the outskirts or to smaller communities. Our larger cities have become so overcrowded that there is little hope of making the districts near their centers suitable places for family residence. Perhaps the most important cause of this overcrowding has been the concentration of industries and other large employers of labor. Now that the industries are finding it advantageous to move out it is not only possible to provide much better houses for their employees in the more sparsely settled districts to which they go, but also it will prove easier to raise standards in the old districts as the pressure of population diminishes.

The most difficult phase of the urban housing problem is land overcrowding. During the past generation this has been steadily increasing. Rapid transit, while it has aided in spreading population has also had no inconsiderable effect in concentrating population by making the city center more accessible to those living at a distance. The big store which draws its patronage from widely scattered suburbs has hundreds of employees who cannot afford the time or the money to live beyond walking distance. To them and to others whose work must be carried on downtown the removal of the industries with their armies of employees means the possibility of better living.

But so far the heads of most of the migrating industries have failed to make full use of the opportunities presented by their new locations. Their thoughts, apparently, have been almost exclusively for the plant, only incidentally, if at all, for the operatives. These have been left to shift for themselves. Even so, conditions improved. For in spite of apparent examples to the contrary the factory tends to draw its workers after it and so out of the crowded city center and into the more spacious suburbs. But this is not enough, as some of our leaders have begun to clearly see. Left to the automatic working of supply and demand the new industrial districts will soon become quite as objectionable as are the old.

During the past few years we have learned a great deal about city building — the results of past neglect have forced us to learn. The removal of the factories themselves is a case in point, even as the well-planned factory is a fair analogy to what the well-planned city should be. Such removals when due to preventable causes constitute a tremendous economic waste. Are we to repeat them again in a few years? A similar waste is going on in the residence districts of our American cities, which, because of lack of proper planning and protection, lose in market values at the rate of hundreds of millions of dollars a year. This is the statement of a well-known real-estate man who estimates that in his own city alone the preventable loss to blighted residence districts is several million dollars a year.

So the founding of these new industrial suburbs comes at a time when past experience and present study fit us to make them far better communities than the old. We can prevent the repetition there of the old land crowding. We can make them communities of homes, with all that this means in better health, higher moral and social standards, increased efficiency. But to accomplish this means thought and effort. The head of the factory does not believe that his new buildings will be grouped so as to assure the greatest economy of operation unless he plans them carefully. To let the head of each department arrange matters to suit himself without consulting the heads of other departments would not result in efficiency for the plant as a whole. Nor will the new town provide as it should for its varied functions if each is considered separately by different groups of men.

The old theory that the employer has no interest in what goes on outside his factory walls has been exploded. He has not only interest but responsibility, for he is by virtue of his industrial position a man of influence in the community. What it becomes will reflect with fair accuracy what kind of man he is.

INDEX